D1288213

Charles University
Karolinum Press

PRAGUE

THE CITY AND ITS RIVER

Kateřina Bečková

Photographs by Věroslav Škrabánek
Translated by Derek and Marzia Paton

Karolinum Press

Originally published in Czech as Praha – Město a řeka, Prague: Karolinum, 2015
KAROLINUM PRESS, Ovocný trh 560/5, 116 36 Prague 1, Czech Republic
Karolinum Press is a publishing department of Charles University in Prague
www.karolinum.cz

Edited by Milada Motlová (Czech) and Martin Janeček (English)
Cover and graphic design by Zdeněk Ziegler
Typeset by DTP Karolinum
Printed in the Czech Republic by EUROPRINT, a. s., Praha
First English edition
ISBN 978-80-246-3292-6

The manuscript was reviewed by Jan Jungmann, PhDr (City of Prague Museum),
and Josef Štulc, PhDr (National Heritage Institute, Prague)

The Prague series is edited by Milada Motlová

CONTENTS

THE CITY AND ITS RIVER

From riverside settlement to city

A river flowing through a town always remains part of nature, no matter how much it seems to have completely extricated itself from all the natural elements and become a tamed part of human settlement. For centuries it can be a faithful servant to the city that grows up on its banks, and can provide it with energy, charm, and a living, and yet it surprises us again and again with its unexpected rebelliousness when it emphatically reminds everyone of its wild natural essence.

Prague was gradually built up on the welcoming terrain of the basin in which the mostly narrow valley of the River Vltava broadens between the cliff at Vyšehrad and the meander at Holešovice. Here, the river overflowed its banks and became wider and shallower, and thus, in the early history of this settlement, it provided an easy ford for merchants travelling the long routes from east to west and west to east. The area near the ford thus became a crossroads that naturally attracted settlement. No one today really knows exactly where the original ford was located, but it is reasonable to assume that it lay in the area between what is today Klárov and a section of the Aleš Embankment in the Old Town. In fact, the location of the ford could have slightly changed from time to time, depending on the natural conditions of the river, which created quickly changing little islands, shallows, and pools after the frequent floods. There is strong evidence, however, that the ford on the Old Town side originated in the extended direction of the original street today called Kaprova, because it was at one specific point here where five roads running from the south, east, and north met, as is shown by the historical plan of the built-up area of the Old Town before the slum clearance of the late nineteenth and the early twentieth century.

It took a long time, however, for the city to subdue the river. From the settled land near the riverbank Prague became a real city only once the increasingly dense built-up areas made it necessary to link the two banks by means of the first bridge. In the Prague basin this turning point occurred in the tenth century at the latest, which we know from a fragmentary report about the existence of a wooden bridge here. The lifespan of the bridge, however, was limited by big floods, and a monumental stone bridge was built here instead from 1158 to 1172. It was called the Judith Bridge in honour of its initiator and protector, Judith of Thuringia, the queen consort of King Vladislav II. But even this bond of stone was only temporary, and after almost two hundred years of service it was shaken off by the river in the great flood of 1342. Its successor was the Charles Bridge, originally called the Stone Bridge, founded, with unshakeable faith in the power of the stars and protective symbols, by Charles IV at 5:31 am (dawn), on 9 July 1357. At its birth, the bridge was thus given a protective wall of rising and falling odd numbers, 1–3–5–7–9–7–5–3–1, which, despite countless attacks by the water, seems to have

JORIS HOEFNAGEL AND ABRAHAM HOGENBERG, *View of Prague from 1572*, hand-coloured copper engraving, from *Civitates orbis terrarum* (1598).

View from Letná looking towards the Prague basin with the historic core of the city, which the Vltava flows past in an irregular semicircle.

protected it to this day. Nevertheless, the bridge is no longer quite the authentic Gothic construction it was in Charles's day, because it has undergone many repairs, particularly after being damaged by floods in 1784 and 1890.

Flowing through Prague directly from south to north, the river runs into the rocky formation of Letná along its left bank, and turns at a right angle towards the east, thus flowing in an irregular semi-circle past the Prague basin, which contains the historic core of the town. So, apart from the Castle district (Hradčany), all the historic towns of Prague – the Old Town, the New Town, and the Lesser Town – are in direct contact with the river.

The river as an energy source

Before they gradually discovered other beneficial uses for water power, people first used rivers for fishing, bathing, and washing clothes. Beginning in the Middle Ages, flour mills were built on the riverbanks, but so too were other enterprises that used waterwheels to provide power for the mechanical tasks of trade and, later, manu-facturing. In addition to flour mills, people soon built plants for stone-cutting and stone-grinding, saw mills, hammer mills, as well as paper mills, tanneries, taweries (tanneries using a dry process), dye-works, and bleacheries, using water as a raw material or to provide power. For its successful operation, each water-powered ma-chine usually needs to increase the flow rate of the river and the mass of the water power, and that's why weirs have been built on the river. Weirs artificially raise the water level and divert part of the seemingly lazy flow to a mill race, where the fall-ing water or quickened current turns a waterwheel.

For almost their whole length the banks of the historic Prague towns were used for trade. That meant that people could not walk along them as we can today. One could go down to the river mostly where the landings were. Other parts of the banks were covered with buildings that created something like the 'industrial

RUDOLF ALT AND F. X. SANDMANN, *At the Old Town Mills*, hand-coloured lithograph, *c.*1840.

The landing at the Old Town Mills was the liveliest place of contact between the townspeople and the river. On the right, the Old Town Mills and Water Tower.

BEDŘICH HAVRÁNEK, *Between the New Mills and the Helm Mills*, watercolour, *c.*1850.

Every part of the riverside of the Vltava downstream at Mayor's Island (Primátorský ostrov), in the New Town, was fully exploited for business. In the background, the New Mills Water Tower.

VÁCLAV KROUPA, **Sand Miners Upstream from the Šítka Weir**, oil on canvas, 1884.

The Šítka Water Tower with its typical onion dome; in the foreground, sand miners and their little barges, dredging sand from the riverbed.

zones' of the historic towns. Until the mid-nineteenth century the economic use of the riverbanks at Prague was of prime importance; not until the spread of steam engines was production gradually brought further inland and the river, at least in the centre of town, was freed up for new tasks and possibilities.

The oldest Prague weir is the Old Town Weir (Staroměstský jez), dating from the thirteenth century. Though it has been repaired many times since then and was shortened a hundred years ago by the width of a navigable canal on its left bank, the weir has kept the original direction between the Sova Mills and the Old Town Mills. The smooth surface of the water it holds back creates the characteristic Prague mirror in which is reflected Hradčany together with the Charles Bridge and, from the other side, the landmarks of the Old Town riverbank. But in addition to this widely appreciated aesthetic effect, the Old Town Weir led to considerable complications for the further use of the river, since, together with the numerous other weirs by mills of the New Town, both upstream and downstream, it created a barrier to uninterrupted river traffic through the centre of town. This barrier was not surmounted until the beginning of the twentieth century. Previously, the river was navigable only for rafts and light cargo vessels that sailed through the shallow sluice of the weir, whose building and maintenance were among the miller's fundamental responsibilities.

Water towers, fountains, and cisterns
For a long time after the riverbanks had begun to become densely settled and could be classified as towns, the inhabitants made due in their everyday lives with water from their own wells and with water from the many natural sources, which was

SALOMON EMANUEL FRIEDBERG-MÍROHORSKÝ, *The Riverbank at Smíchov Upstream from the Lesser Town Waterworks*, oil on canvas, 1886.

The Petržilka Tower of the Lesser Town Waterworks seen from a path on the riverside at Smíchov.

often conducted by gravity through simple wooden pipes or carried from the river. From its beginning, for example, the Strahov monastery built a simple water-supply system that caught the water from the slopes of Petřín Hill. Similarly, Vyšehrad and Prague Castle met their water needs each in their own way.

The water of the Vltava could be used efficiently in the town only once technology had been developed which would enable the construction of a pump to conduct water into a tank in a tower, from which, by the force of gravity, it would then flow to where it was to be used, that is, public fountains and the cisterns and fountains of palaces, convents and monasteries, and other private houses. In the mid-seventeenth century, for example, the Old Town waterworks alone supplied about a hundred cisterns. The power for drawing the water was generated by water-wheels, which, much like mill wheels, were turned by the force of the river current. The waterworks stood beside the tower. Water towers were therefore naturally built near mills and, together with them, used the waterheads of the Prague weirs. The first in Prague was the Old Town Water Tower next to the Charles Bridge at the Old Town Mills. Evidence of the existence of what was probably a wooden tower on that site dates from 1489. The stone tower, which still stands, dates from 1577, though it has frequently been rebuilt after numerous fires and wars. Not only were fires often caused by neglect of people employed at the water-supply facilities while working with open flames, like candles and heaters, but the towers, rising high above the river, were also easy targets for gunners during the sieges of Prague. The Old

ALTSTÄDTER RING.

Prag bei Borrosch et André.

VINCENC MORSTADT AND VÁCLAV MERKLAS,
The Krocín Fountain, steel engraving, 1847.

Together with the Marian column, the big
Krocín Fountain, from the late sixteenth century,
was a landmark of Old Town Square.

Town Water Tower, for example, was damaged in 1648 by Swedish cannon, in 1756
by Prussian cannon, and in 1848 by the guns of the Austrian Imperial garrisons led
by the unpopular General Windischgrätz against the rebelling people of Prague.

South of the Old Town Waterworks, the New Town Water Tower and waterworks
were built in 1495, and soon came to be named after the Šítka Mills next to it. The
original wooden tower was burnt to the ground, and the stone tower erected in
its place, from 1588 to 1591, stands to this day. It was given its now characteristic
onion dome after repairs following Swedish bombardment in 1648.

Another New Town water tower, also originally made of wood, was erected
upstream at the New Mills (Nové mlýny), in 1536, and has therefore ever since
been called the New Mills Tower (Novomlýnská věž). After a fire, a stone tower
was built, from 1602 to 1606, to replace it, but that was destroyed by wood and ice
carried downstream in the flood of 1655. The new stone tower, which still stands
on this spot, dates from 1658.

The fourth Prague water tower, the Malostranská vodárenská věž, belongs to the
Lesser Town, though it was erected beyond the town walls at the weir on a small
island next to the Petržilka Mill (Petržilkovský mlýn), and is sometimes therefore
still called the Petržilkovská věž. Its earliest wooden structure, from 1502, was replaced before 1596 by a masonry structure, which is preserved to this day.

At the Museum of the Prague Water Supply (Muzeum pražského vodárenství) one can see the original seventeenth-century plans for the distribution of water from Prague water towers, from which one can discern where the pipelines ran through the city and where the supply points were. Probably the most famous public fountain in Prague was the Krocín Fountain (Krocínova kašna) on Old Town Square (Staroměstské náměstí), named after its builder, a mayor of the Old Town, Václav Krocín z Drahobejle. This outstanding work of sculpture with a number of delicately executed allegorical figures of red marble from Slivenec (now part of greater Prague) was made by an unknown artist from 1591 to 1596. Periods of war and political instability in subsequent centuries led to the neglect of the water pipelines: the wooden pipes were not caulked or became clogged or both, and the stone cisterns leaked or overflowed. The famous Krocín Fountain also suffered from such neglect, and was removed from the square in 1862. What remains of it is exhibited at the Lapidarium of the National Museum on the Exhibition Grounds (Výstaviště). Other large fountains were later removed from the centres of squares because they no longer served their original purpose and obstructed tramways.

Another famous source of water in Prague was the Wimmer Fountain, a copy of which today stands in the middle of the Coal Market (Uhelný trh) in the Old Town. This charming fountain, with water gushing from the beak of a swan and with an allegorical girl and boy, was made by the sculptor František Xaver Lederer in 1797, on a commission from a rich burgher called Jakub Wimmer, originally for the little square on the Nové aleje, now Národní třída (National Avenue).

Equally well-known and beloved is the fountain popularly known as Terezka (Little Theresa), built into the wall of the Clam-Gallas House on Mariánské náměstí. The statue of a girl holding two jugs is an allegory of the River Vltava. One jug, from which flows a strong stream of stone, represents the main flow of the river. The second jug, from which water freely gushes into the basin, symbolizes the waterworks supplying the town. The statue was made by the sculptor Václav Prachner in 1812, based on a design by Josef Bergler. According to legend, a retired captain of the dragoons, who lived nearby, fell in love with the delightful stone girl and made her one of his heirs in his last will and testament. The original of the sculpture is now in the National Gallery.

In Husova ulice (Hus Street), near the Terezka Fountain, one can look into the courtyard of the Clam-Gallas House and see a Baroque fountain like those that used to be installed on the courtyards of the houses of the nobility. This particular fountain is decorated with a sculpture of the sea god Triton by Matthias Bernhard Braun from 1716.

For more than four centuries, the four Prague waterworks and their towers were enough to supply Prague with water. When the machinery became old, it was improved and modernized, and, beginning in the first half of the nineteenth century, the wooden pipes were replaced with cast iron ones. From 1880 onward the historic water towers were gradually taken out of service. At that time, water power had already for a few decades ceased to be used to drive the machines, and new steam or electric waterworks machinery with a greater capacity provided Prague with water. From 1906 to 1913 a joint waterworks was built in the village of Kárané to supply Prague and its neighbouring municipalities. Since that time, the people of Prague no longer use Vltava water for their households.

WILHELM RUPP, *Podskalí from the North*, photograph, *c.*1865.

The earliest photo of the riverbank at Podskalí, still with the Baroque silhouette of the Basilica of St Peter and St Paul at the top of Vyšehrad and still without the iron bridge.

Podskalí and timber rafting

One settlement below Vyšehrad Rock (Vyšehradská skala) stood out from the others on the Prague banks of the Vltava by the kind of business that was conducted here. Called Podskalí, it was the centre of raftsmen and timber merchants. The earliest records of its existence date from 1199. It became part of the New Town, which was founded in 1348. The people of Podskalí made their living solely by work linked with the river. Landowners on the riverbank had the right to operate rafting and to trade in timber. That's why the main street of Podskalí had buildings only on one side; the second side was formed by the riverbank with access to the water and timber yards. The best homes in Podskalí were those of the rafters. Wood and other goods were transported by raft from south Bohemia to Prague. The rafts were dismantled in Prague at wharves near where the Botič stream empties into the Vltava. It was here that customs duties were exacted in the form of a certain number of logs, initially to the benefit of the collegiate church of Vyšehrad and then, from the mid-fifteenth century to 1771, to the New Town, and eventually to the state. In 1829, customs duties were lifted, but the place is still called Výtoň (derived from the Czech word *vytínat*, referring to a customs payment in the form of cutting out every twelfth log). By chance, the only noteworthy Podskalí house that has survived is the customs house, in which the Podskalí Museum is now located. After the payment of the customs duty, the logs from the dismantled rafts were hauled up onto the riverbank, dried, debarked, decked and sawn. Trade in timber for building, fuel, and manufacturing then took place in these yards. As is evident from old prints, paintings, and photographs of the town, strings of rafts chained together were anchored in several rows at the upper bank of the New Town, or below Vyšehrad, at Smíchov, or further up the river, before their turn came to be processed. The rafts were a permanent feature of this part of town. Only a smaller number of them were intended to float through the raft sluices of the Prague weirs and on to the narrower section of the river, where some ended up and were reassembled at the wharves called Na Františku. Others continued on. During floods, rafts anchoring at Podskalí and elsewhere above the Prague weirs became a threat to the town centre and especially to Charles Bridge. Indeed, it was the accumulated timber from runaway rafts and flooded timber yards which caused jams under Charles Bridge during the one-hundred-year floods of 1784 and 1890, and, with the accumulated force of the water, broke through it like a battering ram.

After the 1783 letters patent of Joseph II, the rafting and timber trades were not burdened by a monopoly of the Podskalí raftsmen and became a trade for which one did not require certification of qualifications, but the strong tradition continued to concentrate this activity in Podskalí for a least another century. Not until the end of the nineteenth century was it decided to build 1500-metre-long raft moorings at Smíchov (that is, across the river), by partly digging away the riverbank and deepening the river plain. Thus was born the island called Císařská louka (Emperor's Mead), which was originally only a low part of the mainland. The moorings, built

Podskalí from the South, photograph, *c.*1900, unknown photographer.

Podskalská třída (Podskalí Avenue) with the houses of people who owned businesses related to the river and with moored rafts, in a view from the Railway Bridge to the Palacký Bridge. In the foreground on the right, the building of the Podskalí customs house at Výtoň with wharves.

JINDŘICH ECKERT, *Ice Harvesting*,
photograph, *c.*1895

Harvesting ice from the surface of the Vltava
was not only a traditional winter occupation
of the people of Podskalí, but also a popular
spectacle for the people of Prague.

from 1899 to 1903, facilitated work, providing shelter for as many as 200 rafts, but
could accommodate considerably more when Prague was threatened by floods.

The people of Podskalí, however, took other jobs connected with the river and
water in general. They mined sand from the riverbed, harvested ice in winter for
brewers and butchers, and fished, and they also made skating rinks for fun in winter.

Barges and ferries

Apart from rafts, the historic paintings and prints of cityscapes show shallow-draft
cargo vessels on the river. Among them, from 1550 on, were boats carrying salt
from the imperial salthouse in České Budějovice (Budweis), because the right to
buy salt wholesale and then to trade in it was held in Prague exclusively by the
municipality. On the right bank of the river, not far from the customs house at
Výtoň, was the so-called royal salthouse in Podskalí. Further down the river was
the New Town salthouse, on the site of which the National Theatre was later built.
And even further down the river, where the Smetana Embankment (Smetanova
nábřeží) is today, stood the Old Town salthouse where the Bellevue is today. Apart
from salt, barges carried mainly potatoes, grain, vegetables, and other foodstuffs,

(22)

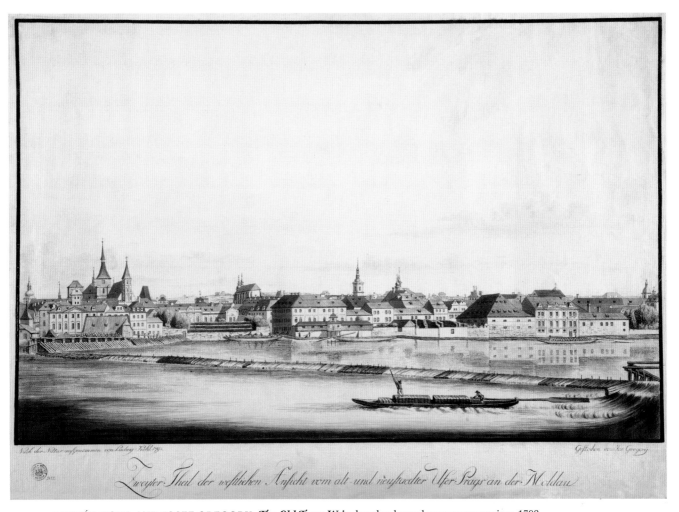

Zweyter Theil der westlichen Ansicht vom alt- und neustaedter Ufer Prags an der Moldau

LUDVÍK KOHL AND JOSEF GREGORY, *The Old Town Weir*, hand-coloured copper engraving, 1793.

The Old Town Weir with a log sluice, which a shallow-draft boat with its cargo has just passed through. In the background, the still unregulated riverbank of the Old Town with the landmark salthouse.

but also sand, cut timber, rubble, and other stone, for example cobbles for Prague streets. But even these shallow-draft vessels, sometimes dozens of feet long, were able to sail through raft sluices. If they were carrying goods from south Bohemia, they generally did not sail farther than the wharves at Na Františku above the Helmovský jez (Helm Weir). Similarly, they had to go over two weirs in the centre of town, the Šítkovský and the Staroměstský. It was also then necessary to tow the vessel through the weirs against the current, which was done either through the narrow lock by means of rope wound around a wheel driven by manpower, or by means of a windlass through the raft sluice. Further on, against the current, the vessel had to be towed by horses on riverside towpaths. Because of other weirs, river transit through Prague and then farther on the lower course of the Vltava was so technically difficult and time-consuming that using it ceased to make commercial sense. Merchants from south Bohemia therefore found it more profitable to sell their vessels in Prague together with their goods. Merchants from north Bohemia and Germany bought vessels in Prague, and had them towed empty downstream, loaded them with goods bought in Prague, and sailed northwards home. Cargo

Karlín Port, oil on canvas, *c*.1850, unknown artist.

View looking towards the Karlín Port, which was established in 1822 for barges on the lower Vltava. On the left, the greenery of the Jerusalem and Rohan islands; on the right, buildings on Pobřežní ulice (Riverside Drive).

that was destined for Prague along the Vltava from the other side, that is, from the north against the current, was unloaded before reaching Prague, either in Bubeneč or, years later, in the river port in Karlín, which was built in 1822. (Like Bubeneč, Karlín became a Prague district in 1922.) Not until 1865 was a steam tugboat used to tow cargo vessels against the current, where the river was deep enough and calm enough to do so. Until the canalization of the Vltava in the late nineteenth and the early twentieth century most of the towing was done by horses. In favourable winds this hard work was made easier by rigging the vessels.

Not only rafts and cargo vessels sailed the river in the centre of town; ferries did too. Although passage on the river was considered open to everyone, before the merger of the Prague towns in 1784 most of the rights connected with river use in the city belonged to the Old Town, as did the right to operate or hire ferries. Since the Middle Ages three ferries had been in operation in the section of the Vltava between Vyšehrad Rock and Holešovice. The first of them sailed from Podskalí, linking it with Smíchov, and remained in service until the building of the Palacký Bridge in 1878. The upper Old Town ferry, with a stop on the northern tip

The Na Františku Wharves, photograph, *c.*1865, unknown photographer.

Barges moored at the Na Františku wharves. They had probably sailed from south Bohemia with goods. They were sold here empty, and could then sail north, downstream, with other goods.

of Sharpshooter Island (Střelecký ostrov) linked the south part of Kampa Island with the Old Town and remained in service until after the completion of the Francis I Chain Bridge in 1841. The lower Old Town ferry linked the area of what is today Klárov with Jan Palach Square (náměstí Jana Palacha). It too went out of business when a new, iron bridge was built on this site in 1868. Other ferries could be used to sail around Vyšehrad Rock, for getting to and from the islands, and of course to navigate the river outside the city centre, for example, downstream at Troja and Holešovice and upstream at Podolí. Operating a ferry was a highly profitable business, which is why the sons of ferrymen followed in their fathers' footsteps and also why we have records of ferrymen's naive protests against the building of bridges.

Building bridges and using islands

Although the Vltava was from time immemorial so important in the settlement of Prague towns, indeed in many respects decisive, for five centuries the people of Prague made due with only one bridge and just a few ferries. A second bridge was built in connection with the grand modern concept of building the first embankment between the Old Town Mills and the Nové lázně (New Baths) opposite Barvířský ostrov (Dyers' Island), renamed at that time Žofín (Sophie's Island, but today officially called Slovanský ostrov, Slav Island, though most people still call it Žofín). The embankment solved the question of what to build at the end of the new bridge on the right bank and it also aimed to create a promenade that afforded a view of Prague Castle with Charles Bridge on the right-hand side and the new Francis I Chain Bridge, the pride of contemporary bridge building, on the left. This bridge, the second in Prague, and the embankment, the first in Prague, were therefore undoubtedly built not only out of the simple need to link the developing Smíchov

JINDŘICH ECKERT, *The Francis I Bridge*, photograph, before 1898.

The Francis I Chain Bridge, looking from Střelecký ostrov to the National Theatre.

FRANTIŠEK FRIDRICH, *The Francis I Bridge*, photograph, *c.*1870.

The second suspension bridge in Prague, it was an elegant structure with Neo-Gothic iron towers.

FRANTIŠEK FRIDRICH, *The Iron Footbridge*, photograph, *c.*1870.

The third suspension bridge in Prague, it ran between Klárov and Rejdiště
(today, náměstí Jana Palacha, that is, Jan Palach Square).

suburb with the centre of Prague, but also to enhance the romantic perception of
the town. This section of the Old Town riverbank, where there had hitherto been a
brickyard, a bleachery, a salthouse, and timber yards, gradually ceased to be used
by tradesmen, and instead began to be appreciated as the place affording the most
impressive views of the panorama of Prague Castle. The whole monumental work,
the bridge and the embankment, was financed by the Bohemian estates and other
provincial funding of the Bohemian Lands. The project involved the urban planning of the whole built-up area of the embankment. It included finding a dignified
site for the monument to the late Francis II, the last Holy Roman Emperor (*reg.*
1792–1806) and the first Emperor of Austria (as Francis I, *reg.* 1804–35), which is a
sculptural composition called *The Homage of the Bohemian Estates* (1850), combining
an equestrian statue of the emperor with a fountain. The sculpture is the work of
Josef Max and the architectural features of the monument are by Joseph Kranner
and is usually called the Kranner Fountain. The whole project of the embankment
and the bridge was the first of many changes that gradually gave the river the appearance we know today.

The technical beauty of the chain bridge was particularly appreciated during the
industrial boom beginning in the mid-nineteenth century, and it encouraged the
city council of Prague to build another two chain suspension bridges. The rampart

road, which is today called Revoluční třída, was linked with the new road below Letná hill by the Francis Joseph I Bridge. The carriageway of the bridge was supported by two cast-iron Neo-Gothic towers on stone piers in the riverbed. The link between Klárov and what is now Palach Square (which at the time was merely an undeveloped area called Rejdiště) was provided by the simple Iron Footbridge. The ten bridges which today span the Vltava between Vyšehrad and Holešovice were all built within a hundred years. Three bridges later replaced the chain bridges that were nearing the end of their lives, and two were built for the railway.

The five islands of Prague which today adorn the surface of the river in the historic centre of town – Kampa, Slovanský (Slav), Střelecký (Sharpshooter), Dětský (Children's), and Štvanice (Blood-sport) – were all created by fluvial deposits in places where the river was shallow, wide, and freely overflowed its banks. Some of the islands that were thus created later vanished without a trace during later flooding; others became bigger and were subsequently shored up by human effort and used for farming, trades, and recreation. In the seventeenth century and at the beginning of the eighteenth, Štvanice had a special function. An arena was built here, in which gory fights were held between game and packs of dogs. This pastime gave the island the name it has today, although, because of the whole group of neighbouring islands along the riverbank at Karlín, it was also called Velké Benátky (Venice). Apart from the main island, the islands that made up the Štvanice group vanished during the regulation of the river and the building of the embankments. Malé Benátky (Little Venice) was a name for Střelecký ostrov (Sharpshooter Island), which was also surrounded by the smaller Slovanský and Dětský islands. This trio of islands is beautifully reflected in the surface of river between the Old Town Weir and the Šítka Weir. The chief aesthetic feature of these islands, enhancing the panoramic views, consists in their many trees and gentle banks.

In the first half of the nineteenth century, inns and dance halls were built at Žofín, Střelecký ostrov, and Štvanice, and became popular destinations for the people of Prague, even though they could only be reached by ferry.

The beginnings of Prague steam navigation
The need to find a cheap means of transporting imperial salt gave the impetus to efforts to use the Vltava as a regular waterway from south Bohemia to Prague. The first work to make it navigable was undertaken between Budweis (České Budějovice) and Prague as early as 1547. Three years later, vessels began carrying salt to Prague salthouses and would continue to do so for more than three centuries. From the mid-nineteenth century onwards, particularly in connection with the beginnings of steamboat traffic, people involved in shipping started to plan for continuous navigation on the Vltava in Prague between the upper and the lower course, which, because of the numerous weirs here, had previously been only a pipe dream. It was, however, a matter of moving not only freight but also people. The first steamboat to sail on the Vltava here was built in a Prague suburb.

It was two Englishmen, the shipper John Andrews and the shipbuilder Joseph John Ruston, who sought to begin regular passenger transport by boat between Prague and Dresden. Following on from Ruston's plans, and with considerable interest from the people of Prague, a third Englishman, Edward Thomas, built a factory on the riverbank at Karlín in 1841, and soon launched the steamboat *Bohemia*.

Das erste Moldau-Dampfboot Bohemia.

Album für Litteratur Kunst und Wißenschaft.

The First Steamboat on the Vltava, lithograph, 1841, unknown artist.
The first steamboat on the Vltava was built in the factory of Joseph John Ruston,
in what is now the Prague district of Libeň. It sailed out on a trial run along the riverbank
at Karlín on 19 May 1841.

This and other steamboats then began a regular Prague–Dresden service, even though they could sail to Prague (actually to Podbaba, north of the city centre) only when the water was high enough. Most of the journeys actually began at Obříství near Mělník, to where the passengers were taken by horse-drawn coach. Although this steamboat business was successful, Ruston closed it down in 1850. He bought Thomas's factory (on the boundary of Karlín and Libeň), which from that time on was popularly known as Rustonka, and he concentrated on designing and building boats.

In 1857, August Winter, a riverboat captain on the Elbe, tried to introduce steamboat service further up the Vltava, between Prague and the town of Štěchovice, about 20 km south. But this business venture was a flop, probably because of the costly rebuilding and repair of an older steamboat imported from Magdeburg. And, unfortunately, he chose to call his steamboat after a disliked governor of Bohemia, Karl von Mecséry, whom he probably had hoped to flatter, not suspecting that this would be publicly unpopular. Moreover, he did not know how treacherous the river was at this particular stretch. On its maiden voyage, the steamboat *Mecséry* ran aground on the shallows and the VIP passengers had to be taken ashore in the punts of local fishermen. The accident was soon repeated while turning around at Vrané on the Vltava, and the damaged steamboat had to return to Prague carried along by the current. And thus ended one shipping enterprise.

After these experiences the river was canalized to ensure the safety of the shipping routes on the stretch from Prague to Štěchovice. The work was carried out by Vojtěch Lanna, a shipbuilder, owner of a large construction company (largely responsible for the Smetana Embankment too), and the holder of a state concession for regulation and maintenance work on the Vltava and the Elbe. On the initiative of František Dittrich, a native of Podskalí, a raftsman, successful timber merchant, and, later, even Mayor of Prague, the Prague Steamboat Company (Pražská společnost pro paroplavbu na řece Vltavě or, today, Pražská paroplavební společnost) was established in 1865. Its shareholders included many Prague businessmen and industrialists, including Lanna and Ruston. The company then built its first steamboat,

JINDŘICH ECKERT, *The Steamboat* **Praha/Prag**, photograph, 1865.

The first steamboat of the Prague Steamboat Company, the *Prag/Praha* was intended for sailing on the upper Vltava. It was built on the landing at Smíchov from parts produced in the Karlín factory popularly known as the Rustonka. In the background, Podskalí and Emmaus Abbey (with its Baroque steeples).

F. J. TROJAN, *The Steamboat* **Primátor Dittrich**, photograph, *c.*1908.

This famous steamboat of the Prague Steamboat Company, the *Primátor Dittrich* is shown here sailing by Vyšehrad Rock, with the Basilica of St Peter and St Paul after its Neo-Gothic remodelling.

the *Prag*, at Ruston's shipyard in Libeň. It was launched on the Vltava at Prague on 26 August 1865. Ruston's shipyard also supplied other steamboats to the company, but because the river between Libeň and New Town was unnavigable, the boats had to be transported in pieces overland by horse-drawn carriage through Prague and over Charles Bridge, and then assembled at the landing in Smíchov, from where they were then launched. The Prague Steamboat Company, unlike its predecessor, succeeded. The people of Prague began to love boat trips, and, except in periods of economic depression and war, the company was so successful that even attempts by the competition to provide sightseeing cruises on a similar route or between the Prague weirs proved to be no threat. The vessels of the Prague Steamboat Company have been cruising the Vltava for a 150 years now. During that time, of course, many boats have come and gone, and some have changed their names more than once owing to political and other circumstances. Today, two steam paddleboats are the flagships of the fleet. They can be admired on their regular voyages up and down the river or at the quays below the Palacký Bridge. The *Vyšehrad* steamboat (originally called the *Antonín* Švehla, then, beginning in 1942, the *Karlstein*, from 1945 on, the *T. G. Masaryk*, renamed the *Děvín* in 1952, and since 1992 the *Vyšehrad*) was built at the shipyard in Ústí nad Labem in 1938; the steamboat *Vltava* was built in the shipyard in Libeň in 1940. Both historic vessels have been restored and, since 2013, are registered as part of the Czech cultural heritage.

Making the Vltava navigable in Prague
But we have run a bit ahead of our story of the city and its river, and therefore have to return to the moment that was decisive in making the Vltava completely navigable

JAROSLAV BRUNER-DVOŘÁK, *At the Smíchov Lock*, photograph, 1931.

The regulation of the banks of the Dětský and Petržilkovský islands was carried out in connection with the building of the Smíchov lock. The strikingly shaped wooden footbridge, which led from the mainland to the island, was later substituted for by a concrete bridge.

JAN NOVOTNÝ, *Sand Barges*, photograph, *c.*1955.

Barges carrying sand, moored at the Ludvík Svoboda Embankment (originally
the St Peter Embankment). Barges were a common sight on the river in the third quarter
of the twentieth century.

in Prague. It was in 1896, when the Bohemian Commission for the Canalization
of the Rivers Vltava and Elbe was set up. Among its tasks was to find a solution to
the Prague problem. A plan was drawn up by the commission. Construction work
began in 1897 with the lock below Prague at Troja and then the navigable canal to
Podbaba. The work therefore first concentrated on the lower course of the Vltava,
to ensure sufficiently safe cargo shipping, which was meant to continue against the
current all the way to the Karlín Commercial Port (Karlínský obchodní přístav), or
to the new, more modern port at Holešovice. Making navigable the section running
through the centre of town was intended mainly for the passenger transport of the
Prague Steamboat Company on the route from the wharf below the Palacký Bridge
to the town of Mělník and then farther down the Elbe. Building work was carried
out on the river beginning in 1909. The first step was to replace two historic weirs,
the Helm Weir and the New Town Weir, with a new Helm Weir and by rebuilding
the Šitka Weir. The main constructions, however, were two locks: the first, built between Štvanice island and the riverbank at Karlín, from 1907 to 1912, was intended
to surmount the height of the new Helm Weir; the second, built between Dětský
ostrov and the riverbank at Smíchov, from 1913 to 1921, surmounts two weirs at
the same time, the Šitka and Old Town Weirs. The work took about fifteen years,
not only because of slowdowns during the First World War, but also because of
the widely and thoroughly debated search for a solution that would not disturb the
appearance of the traditional panorama of Prague around Charles Bridge and the
base of the Prague Castle area. The planners and builders must be given credit for
the tasteful design that was ultimately chosen: the technical part is entirely hidden
from observers on the Smetana Embankment, thanks to the trees of the Dětský and
Střelecký islands. The small lock at the southern tip of Slovanský ostrov, moreover,

The Palacký Embankment, photograph, *c*.1879, unknown photographer.

The newly built Palacký Embankment (today, the Rašín Embankment), still without
a lower level, resembled fortifications. The land behind it was lowered to the original height
of the riverbank at Podskalí. The panorama is dominated by the steeples of Emmaus Abbey,
which had been remodelled in the Baroque style.

enables small sightseeing and pleasure vessels to sail on the water that is pooled
behind the Old Town Weir.

Building the embankments

Also connected to the canalization of the river, that is, the regulation of the flow
in the stone walls lining the riverbed, is the building of the Prague embankments.
Though their primary importance was to protect the town from the frequent vagaries
of the river, the new plots on the land that had been raised above the river afforded
extraordinary views and provided unique opportunities for profitable building
ventures. The construction of the Prague embankments was gradual, taking about
ninety years. Work began in 1841, but was most intensive in the fifty years from
1870 to 1920, when the stretches in the centre of town, particularly on the right
bank, were linked together into a continuous riverside road. Though the river was
narrowed in some places by as much as dozens of yards, the riverside plots were
a welcome addition. On the raised level of the new embankments housing was
constructed which was initially intended to be luxurious apartment buildings, but
was later used for ministries and other offices of the Czechoslovak Republic, which
was declared in late 1918.

The earliest Prague embankments, today called the Smetanovo (Smetana),
Janáčkovo (Janáček), and Alšovo (Aleš), and also the north part of the Rašínovo
(Rašín), did not have a lower level and thus seemed like a huge wall between the
people of Prague and their river. The need to have closer contact with the water, and

Josefov, photograph, 1908, unknown photographer.

The Dvořák Embankment, which had just been built, lines the new quarter, after the slum clearance of the historic Jewish Town – Josefov (or Josefstadt in German), of which only the last cluster of low dark houses remains.

not only for recreation, required a new conception for building the later embankments. That conception already counted on having a wide lower level with ramps for easy access for vehicles. The eastern part of the Dvořák Embankment and the southern part of the Rašín Embankment were both built in this way. The historic quay of the Prague Steamboat Company below the Palacký Bridge (today, the north part of the Rašín Embankment was thus, in 1905, also additionally provided with a lower level. Before that time, passengers could only get to the steamboats by descending steep iron steps directly from the embankment. The stone facing of the embankment walls has also changed with time: the earlier sections are usually faced with stone blocks, granite in the lower part, sandstone in the upper; the later sections are usually faced with Cyclopean masonry, which, unlike the earlier sections, no longer seem so austere and fortification-like. During the second half of the nineteenth century the original arched access openings in the embankment walls were no longer needed. They had previously provided fishermen and raftsmen with a direct link between the river and the land beyond the embankment, and during floods they had also provided a place to keep runaway logs that threatened to block the flow of water under the bridges. When, however, in connection with the new houses the land beyond the embankment was increased in height, these access openings became dead-end tunnels, which are now called *kobky*, cells. In the parts of the Rašín Embankment most frequented today, these cells are used as storage spaces for restaurants there.

The housing built on the Prague embankments and the modern bridges that link the left and right banks are showcases of Bohemian architecture ranging from the

SALOMON EMANUEL FRIEDBERG-MÍROHORSKÝ, *The Embankment*, watercolour, 1903.

The first Prague embankment, today called the Smetana Embankment (originally the Old Town Embankment or just the Embankment, and later the Francis Embankment) terminated in the wall at the south end, opposite Žofín Island, with steps which mainly washerwomen and servants used when doing the laundry.

mid-nineteenth century to the years between the two world wars. With regard to urban planning, the Vltava is the backbone of Prague. On it, from south to north and then on its east–west meander, hang the three historic towns of Prague and many of its historic suburbs. The most typical, now even iconic, Prague cityscapes are always views across the river. It is hardly surprising, then, that the developers and contractors sought to build the highest quality, most impressive houses they could on the new embankments. The houses of the Smetana Embankment have a unified Late Neo-Classical design on plans from the late 1830s by the architect Bernhard Grueber. The houses on the Ferdinand Embankment (today, the north part of the Janáček Embankment) in Smíchov, which was built in the mid-1870s with a number of houses in a restrained revival style, were built almost purely as a business venture. The embankments with houses built in the first decade of the twentieth century (on the Rašín Embankment and the south part of the Janáček Embankment) are like an exhibition of the property developers' showiness, achieved with varying degrees of architectural success.

Places for swimming, water sport, and skating

As the river began to be increasingly perceived as a source of hiking and pleasure trips, its previously unknown function as a place for sport started to develop from the mid-nineteenth century onward. If we disregard the fact that many of the people of Prague, particularly those of the lower classes, spontaneously used to go wading on hot days, splashed about, or even swam at the landings and other suitable places around the islands and by the riverside, the first swimming pool in Prague was built below Letná in 1809. It belonged to the military, and shortly after it had opened it was carried away by floods, allegedly also with the uniforms that the swimmers had taken off and put aside, which then became a welcome addition to the wardrobe of the fishermen at Troja. Another swimming place or riverside swimming bath was on Slovanský ostrov (Slav Island), which in those days was still called Barvířský ostrov (Dyers' Island). The well-known Public Swimming Pool (Občanská plovárna) below Letná was established in 1840. Each swimming place usually had a wooden building on land with changing booths and a raft-like structure floating on the river, which facilitated access to the water and provided the swimming area with a boundary. Some riverside baths provided discreet bathing directly from a cubicle. One entered dressed, took of his or her clothes, bathed, and exited as perfectly put together as when he or she had entered.

The swimming baths on the river in the centre of town were closed down in the 1960s and 1970s. A reminder of riverside bathing which still stands today is the elegant building of the Public Swimming Pool below Letná, designed by Joseph Kranner. The charming pavilion with an Empire-style portico flanked by symmetric wings is now a restaurant. As late as after the Second World War, bathing in the Vltava was not at all unusual, and on hot summer days the banks were covered with

PLOVÁRNA OBČANSKÁ
v Praze 1841.

CIVIL-SCHWIMMSCHULE
in Prag 1841.

VINCENC KÜHNEL, *The Public Swimming Pool*, lithograph, 1841.

The Public Swimming Pool in Prague has a riverside building with an elegant Empire-style portico facing the river.

PAVEL KÖRBER, *The Slovanka Swimming Baths*, watercolour, *c.*1900.

The swimming place, called Slovanka, on the bank of Slovanský ostrov (Slav Island),
was in operation until the 1950s.

bathers, particularly in the south of the city, at Podolí and Braník, which is also
where the well-known Žluté lázně (Yellow Baths) and Modré lázně (Blue Baths)
were built.

Another use for the river, more social than sporting, became possible in winter.
Beginning in the mid-nineteenth century, a rink was set up on the surface of the
river, which in those days regularly froze over. After it proved to be a very suitable
pastime during which to make acquaintances, skating increased hugely in popularity. The rink, with refreshments and often also with musical accompaniment, was
usually set up and operated by the people of Podskalí.

Both bathing and skating on the Vltava came to an end with the building of
the dams of the Vltava Cascade, particularly after the building of the Slapy Dam in
1955. On its way to Prague, the cold water released through the dam from a height
of 60 metres does not have enough time to warm up, and remains too cold to bathe
in. In winter, the opposite is true: the water is too warm to freeze. Skating and
bathing of course became no less popular; they simply moved away from the river,
although the best known Prague places for these activities were still close to the
Vltava. An uncovered winter sports stadium with an artificial ice surface had already
been built on Štvanice Island in 1931, encouraged by the success of Czechoslovak
hockey teams, particularly after their victory in the 1929 European Championship.
Four World Ice Hockey Championships took place at Štvanice, in 1933, 1938, 1947,
and 1959, and each time the Czechoslovaks won a medal, including a gold in 1947.
In summer, the stadium was used for basketball, tennis, and other sports. It was
also used as a public skating rink. It was given a wooden roof in 1956. Though the
stadium was listed as a heritage site in 2000, the poor state of its wooden structure
led to its being officially condemned to demolition in 2011.

RUDOLF BRUNER-DVOŘÁK, *Skaters on the Vltava*, photograph, 1905,

Masses of people from Prague skating on the frozen Vltava below Vyšehrad near the just-completed tunnel.

Competitive swimming was given a dignified and beautiful Prague location at the stadium in Podolí. This graceful, mostly glass building was designed by Richard Podzemný, and was erected on the site of a demolished cement works from 1959 to 1965, uniting pre-war Functionalist architecture with the then latest Czechoslovak trend, the Brussels Style (named after the successful Czechoslovak pavilion at Expo 58).

In the second half of the nineteenth century the first rowers appeared on the Vltava. The birthplace of the modern sport of rowing is England and it was Englishmen living in Prague who, in 1860, founded the first rowing club here. Soon after its establishment in 1862, the Sokol physical training association established a rowing club, and the rapidly growing popularity of the sport provided the impetus for the founding of other clubs. By 1905 there were at least ten. For their clubhouses and boathouses they most often used locations on the banks of the river in the direction of Braník and Podolí, later Schwarzenberský ostrov (Schwarzenberg Island, today, Veslařský ostrov) and other islands. The best-known clubs were Regatta (founded in 1870), the Veslařský klub Blesk (the Lightning Rowing Club, founded in 1879), the Veslařský klub Slavia (founded in 1885), and the Český veslařský klub (Bohemian Rowing Club, founded in 1905). The last three named clubs are still active today.

RUDOLF BRUNER-DVOŘÁK, *The Prague Mayor's Eights*, photograph, 1912

The Prague Mayor's Eights (Primátorky) rowing races, in their third year. In the background, the Smíchov brewery and other industries of Smíchov.

The rowers of the individual clubs competed with each other in numerous regattas, of which the Prague Mayor's Eights (Primátorské osmiveslice), first held in 1910, continues to this day.

In carrying on the tradition of rowing in Bohemia, the Water Sports Stadium (Stadion vodních sportů), with an elegant tower for referees and spectators, was built in 1961 on the bank of Císařská louka (Emperor's Mead) for the European Rowing Championship.

Besides sports watercraft propelled by rowers, sailing boats began to appear on the river in the 1870s and 1880s. If the wind was favourable they could daringly overtake the vessels of the Prague Steamboat Company. In 1893, these sailing enthusiasts established the Bohemian Yacht Club (Český Yacht klub), whose seat became, in 1912, the newly erected three-storey wooden building with a boathouse on the levee of the Podolí port (Podolský přístav) below Vyšehrad. The club seat is there to this day, and the unique hundred-year-old building is now a listed heritage site.

In addition to sportsmen and sportswomen organized in clubs, a considerable number of weekend tourists also went in for recreation and occasional water sports, particularly in the golden age of Czech 'tramping' (hiking and camping) in the 1920s and 1930s. The romantic valley of the Vltava upstream from Štěchovice attracted people who built simple cottages and cottage colonies and made camping grounds on its slopes, and a great number of people from Prague flocked there at weekends. Among them were also people willing to have their canoes towed by horses along the towpaths all the way to the Svatojánské proudy (St John Nepomucene Rapids), so that they could then have the pleasure of riding the current back to Prague.

The liking for sojourns in the great outdoors by the river or right on the river took another form as well – namely, cabins built on boats, houseboats. At first the crew also needed to have their floating dwellings towed by horses along the towpaths or, if they could afford it, to have them towed by motorboats. By the 1930s, however, motorized houseboats also appeared, though of course only for the wealthier social classes, who also found a desirable diversion in camping on the water and succumbed to the vogue. In Prague, houseboats were traditionally moored particularly in the Smíchov and the Podolí ports and in Libeň on an arm of the river called the Stará plavba (Old River Route). In addition, motorboating also became more popular. After the Second World War it led to such dense traffic and pollution on the Vltava that for environmental reasons a ban on motorboat traffic on all the Vltava reservoirs was issued in 1976. Though the ban was lifted in 2006, motorboat races are still not permitted on the Vltava.

Prague floods

What I have written so far about the work and recreation of people living on the banks of the Vltava, describing how the river obediently served the town and its needs, may seem to contradict what I stated at the outset – namely, that the river essentially never ceased to be untamed. But it really has never ceased to be wild; it is just that it shows its true nature only every hundred years or so. Consequently, only the fifth or sixth generation has direct experience of its rampaging, once the fourth or fifth generation has completely ceased to believe that the 'legend' of the hundred-year water might reveal itself again sometime.

The Flood of 1872, photograph, 1872, unknown photographer.

Logs, a boat, and a cubicle from a swimming place, which have been carried away by the flood of 25 May 1872, have accumulated in front of Charles Bridge.

The Flood of 1890, photograph, 1890, unknown photographer.

The flood of September 1890 broke through three arches and tore down two piers of Charles Bridge in the main riverbed.

The Flood of 14 August 2002, photograph, 2002, Martin Gust (ČTK).

The view from Štefánik Bridge looking towards the Dvořák Embankment, which is already completely under water. On the Embankment, near the Na Františku Hospital, soldiers, on 14 August, build a levee of sandbags. This, the largest of modern floods, was called a thousand-year water.

The Bearded Man, photograph, 2016, Věroslav Škrabánek.

On the riverside wall by the Monastery of the Knights of the Cross with the Red Star (at Křižovnické náměstí) there is a relief sculpture of the head of bearded man. Called 'Bradáč', it comes from the twelfth-century Judith Bridge. It is said that Bradáč was an index of the water level: if it was completely submerged, that meant that even people on Old Town Square were at least ankle-deep in water.

Even though we knew photographs of the last hundred-year water in Prague in 1890, which broke apart the Charles Bridge, we did not believe the forecasts of the floods in 2002 and we initially went to look at the rising water level as a mere curiosity. When the river forced the authorities to evacuate the riverside localities, and it submerged the Metro (the Prague underground) and hundreds of buildings, the surprised people of Prague began to divide themselves according to whether they lived on the right bank or the left; before then they had never perceived the river as a boundary or obstacle. Though the water in Prague had risen in the twentieth century several times before, those extraordinary events did not reach catastrophic levels and were judged as fifty-year water in 1940 and twenty-year water in 1954. Moreover, after the Vltava Cascade of nine large dams was built, the people of Prague were convinced that the danger of flooding in Prague was thus forever averted because the dams securely held back flood water and the streamflow could be regulated to acceptable rates. But the extreme saturation of the drainage basin of the Vltava was increased in 2002 by heavy rains, which also raised the levels of the Vltava tributaries, that is, the Berounka and the Sázava. Direct experience with the catastrophic flood of 2002 led to the fact that the repeated flood threats to Prague in June 2013 no longer took anyone much by surprise, and the city could successfully try out its crisis plan and build flood walls.

Prague has a rich history of floods. The first authentic record of them is the entry in Cosmas Pragensis's twelfth-century *Chronica Boëmorum*, which notes that in the year 1118 a village on the Vltava was overcome by a flood, 'the likes of which the world had not seen since the Great Deluge'. In an entry for 1342, when a flood swept away the Judith Bridge, the chronicler Francis of Prague lamented: 'when that famous bridge collapsed, it was as if the crown of the kingdom had fallen, and people encountered great difficulty and danger when crossing the river, and the poor were full of sorrow for they could not pay the ferry.' At least one flood is mentioned in the records of every century, but more often several appear. During the last 250 years floods hit Prague in February 1784, when accumulated wood and ice floes caused the sixth pier of Charles Bridge to collapse, together with the sentry post. This was a portent of the surprisingly many assaults on Prague and Charles Bridge by floods in the nineteenth century (in 1824, 1845, 1872, and 1890), to which the bridge ultimately submitted.

The hundred-year water in September 1890 was an extraordinary event for eye-witnesses. They captured it in numerous photographs, focusing particularly on the remains of Charles Bridge, when three arches and two piers in the main riverbed were torn down by the force of water, which had been increased by the mass of runaway rafts and bits of swimming baths. Two sculptural groups by F. M. Bro-koff – St Ignatius of Loyola and St Francis Xavier – were also plunged into the Vltava. The section of the bridge damaged by the flood was quickly replaced by a makeshift wooden construction, and expert bridge-builders became involved in heated discussions with each other about how to restore it. Some argued that instead of the two demolished piers and three arches it would be better to build just one pier and two arches with a larger span, in order to enlarge the depth and velocity profile where the main current flowed. Fortunately, in the interest of preserving the original appearance of the bridge the proposal was rejected. The restoration work took almost a year after the flood, and was completed only in November 1892. Both of the sculptural groups were fished out of the river, but the one of St Ignatius of Loyola was not returned to its place on the bridge. Instead, a sculptural group of the Slav saints Cyril and Methodius, by Karel Dvořák, was installed, in 1938, as the last piece in the sculptural gallery of Charles Bridge.

The Vltava as an inspiration to artists
The Vltava has inspired Bohemian artists working in a range of genres of visual art, literature, and music. The unique musical portrait of the Vltava as the backbone of Bohemia is the symphonic poem 'The Vltava' by Bedřich Smetana, from his cycle *My Country*. It paints in sound the course of the Vltava from its modest source to a stream and then to its becoming a river flowing through the picturesque Bohemian countryside, where people celebrate, fairies and water nymphs dance in meadows, and hilltop castles rise up to the skies. From the wild St John Nepomucene Rapids, the Vltava becomes a mighty river passing the legendary Vyšehrad Rock as it moves towards Prague and continues on majestically into the Elbe. 'The Vltava', doubtless the best known part of the anthem-like cycle *My Country*, was composed in 1874, as its second part, just after the symphonic poem 'Vyšehrad'.

The Vltava as a characteristic symbol of Prague and a source of memory, consolation, and hope is also treated in literature, particularly lyric verse, and is personified in the works of the twentieth-century poet Jaroslav Seifert. It appears as an important Prague location and place of profound mystery also in popular legends and stories.

The most easily accessible depictions are sculptural works on the theme of the Vltava, placed in public spaces, where they can be seen by people walking through

BEDŘICH HAVRÁNEK, *After the Fire*, watercolour, 1848.

A view of the water tower and the Old Town Mills just after a devastating fire.

Prague. We have already looked at the fountain on the allegory of the Vltava, called Terezka, located at Mariánské náměstí. A similar subject, a girl pouring water from a jug, is used in another Vltava allegory, which forms part of the sculptural group *Čechie* on the ramp of the National Museum at the top end of Wenceslas Square. It is a work by the sculptor Antonín Pavel Wagner, from 1889–91. A delightful girl reclines to the right of the central figure of the composition; her counterpart on the left, a male figure, is an allegory of the Elbe. The sculptural group rises above the well-known cascade fountain decorating the front ramps and steps of the Museum. The allegory of the Vltava from 1916, on a high pedestal at the northern tip of Dětský ostrov, is clearly visible from the Janáček Embankment and the Bridge of the Legions. The bronze girl in a theatrical pose has a symbolic little boat at her feet. The figures of four other girls, shown in relief on the lower part of the pedestal, form her retinue. They are allegories of the Vltava tributaries – the Berounka, with a mill wheel, the Otava, with a gold pan, the Sázava, with a fish, and the Lužnice, with a bouquet. The sculpture is by Josef Pekárek; the architectural

WENCESLAUS HOLLAR, *The New Mills Water Tower*, etching, 1636, Národní galerie v Praze.

A view of the New Mills Waterworks as seen from the western tip of Štvanice (Blood-sport) island. As early as the seventeenth century, Hollar, in a series of small etchings of Prague, was depicting the charm of the Vltava with its landmark water towers.

JAKUB SCHIKANEDER, *On the Embankment*, oil on canvas, 1910–20, 84.5 × 107 cm, Národní galerie v Praze.

After 1910, when he chose the life of a recluse, Schikaneder concentrated on night scenes of Prague, capturing the mystery of little streets and remote corners or the melancholy of the banks of the Vltava with an autumnal atmosphere. These paintings are among the best known and most popular of his works.

VÁCLAV PRACHNER, *Allegory of the Vltava (Terezka)*, 1826, photograph, 2016, Věroslav Škrabánek.

The most popular allegory of the Vltava, decorating the fountain at Mariánské náměstí (Marian Square), is popularly known as 'Terezka' (Little/Sweet Theresa). According to popular legend, a certain captain of the dragoons liked this delightful girl of stone so much that he bequeathed her a considerable amount of property. His relations naturally protested, and so Terezka never became rich.

design, connected with the building of the nearby lock chamber and levee, is by František Sander. Every year, on All Souls' Day, a memorial service for the drowned is held at the statue. The largest sculptural gallery of allegorical figures depicting Bohemian rivers, with the Vltava in first place, is located on the south wall of the Podolí Waterworks (Podolská vodárna), a huge building designed by Antonín Engel and built from 1922 to 1929. Above all the other statues stands the sculptor Józa Novák's Vltava, represented by a charming young woman in a baroquely rippling cloak. Below it are the figures of ten girls in the roles of the Vltava tributaries: from the left, the Vydra, the Otava, the Blanice in the Bohemian Forest (Šumava), the Malše, the Berounka, the Sázava, the Blanice (below Blaník Hill), the Želivka, the Lužnice, and the Nežárka. The figures are the work of the sculptors Josef Fojtík, Zdeněk Vodička, and Józa Novák.

The Vltava as a conspicuous, indeed determining, visual feature of the town occurs in all drawings, prints, and paintings of the Prague panorama, beginning with the first known Prague cityscape, from 1493. Letná Hill and Petřín Hill, from which one has a clear view of the Prague basin with the built-up areas of the Prague towns

BEDŘICH SMETANA, *The Vltava*, 1874, title page of the score.

'The Vltava' is the second composition in the cycle of symphonic poems *My Country*, which consists of 'Vyšehrad', 'The Vltava', 'Šárka', 'From Bohemian Meadows and Groves', 'Tábor', and 'Blaník', written from 1874 to 1879. Every year, on 12 May, the anniversary of the composer's death, the Prague Spring Festival opens with this composition.

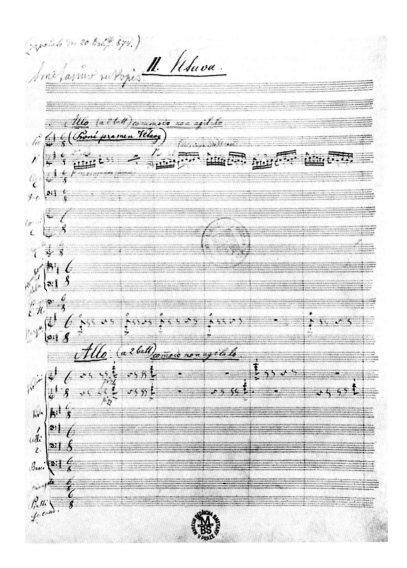

on the river, has inspired many artists to depict the city or parts of it. For example, apart from his large view of Prague from 1636, Wenceslaus (Václav) Hollar, made a number of cityscapes in the second quarter of the seventeenth century, showing the banks of the Vltava with the landmark water towers. The Vltava became a requisite feature of foregrounds and backgrounds, and even the main subject matter, in works by artists of the first half of the nineteenth century – the golden age of the topographically accurate cityscape. The best known of them is undoubtedly the set of watercolours and prints by Vincenc Morstadt, but many other artists of course worked with Prague and the Vltava as their subject matter. The need to depict the city with 'photographic' precision was, beginning in the 1860s, superseded by the photographic cityscape, once and for all freeing the fine arts from the task of documentation. That of course does not mean that works of art eschewed the Vltava, but it does mean that the river ceased to be mere stage scenery and became instead an important subject in paintings of Prague in the twentieth century. And photographs were of course more than mere documents.

The city of Prague and the River Vltava were also paid great artistic tribute by Josef Sudek in his series of panoramic photographs.

JOSEF SUDEK, **Charles Bridge**, 1950s, photograph from the *Panoramic Prague* series.

'Kdo Prahu miluje, / nemůže jinak, / je to tak trochu prokletí.'
(Someone who loves Prague, /Cannot help it. /It's a bit of a curse.)
Jaroslav Seifert, from the poem 'Josef Sudek'.

THE CITY AND ITS RIVER: A GUIDE

1A–D/ VYŠEHRAD ROCK (VYŠEHRADSKÁ SKÁLA)

Much of the earliest Czech mythology, offering explanations for the foundation of the Czech state and the lines of succession of the first Přemyslid rulers, is centred on the mythological seat of the first rulers of Bohemia, located on this cliff above the river. The top of the cliff (Vyšehrad means High Castle) is most likely where the mythological Princess Libuše prophesied the birth of the city of Prague and its future glory. Also according to legend the depths of the Vltava conceal Libuše's treasure, and Libuše's bath was on top of the rock. Also related to Vyšehrad is the legend of Horymír, who was sentenced to death, but then saved by his trusty steed Šemík, who carried him over the Vyšehrad fortifications in a single bound. Respect for the myths surrounding Vyšehrad were once part of every Czech's upbringing, and thus also inspired a number of artists to make important works based on this national tradition.

VYŠEHRAD TUNNEL

The plans to link the town with communities along the south bank by digging a tunnel through Vyšehrad Rock, which was part of building the Vyšehrad (today Podolí) Embankment, was initially considered to be a sign of disrespect for this sacred place. But rational thinking prevailed and a tunnel 32 metres long was built from 1902 to 1905. The tram route did not go through it until 1910. To make the desecration of this cliff more acceptable to the public, the tunnel entrances were decorated with handsome motifs in the style of Romantic fortification architecture, designed by the architect František Velich. He took a similar approach to his design for the little house near the tunnel entrance on the Prague side, which belonged to the official who collected the excise. The embankment wall, intersected by the rocky massive that slopes into the river, is made of Cyclopean masonry with projections of granite ashlars. It lacks a lower level.

VYŠEHRAD

According to legend, Vyšehrad was founded by Krok, the local leader. Regardless of the myths and legends about ancient Bohemia, the fortified settlement at Vyšehrad was built a century after the one at Prague Castle. In the eleventh century, when Vyšehrad briefly became the seat of Vratislav II, the first King of Bohemia, he had it surrounded by ramparts and, in addition, built a palace, two basilicas, and a rotunda. From that point on, Vyšehrad played the role mainly of a spiritual centre, and a number of historical monuments are linked to it. Out of respect to this sacred place of his Přemyslid ancestors, the Emperor and King of Bohemia, Charles IV (1316–1378), not only improved Vyšehrad, but also made it the starting point of the coronation procession of the kings of Bohemia. After its destruction by the Hussites in the fifteenth century, Vyšehrad was eventually, in the seventeenth century, turned into a military fortress, as is evident from its robust ramparts. Czech national feeling in the nineteenth century again focused on Vyšehrad as a symbol of the earliest Czech history.

The originally Romanesque basilica of St Peter and St Paul was founded by Vratislav II in 1070. It was then rebuilt in the Gothic style and later the Baroque, and was given its current appearance as a Neo-Gothic landmark by the architect Josef Mocker. Under his direction, work proceeded from 1885 to 1903 (four years after his death).

(57)

2/ THE VIEW FROM VYŠEHRAD TO PRAGUE CASTLE

An excellent view of the city from Vyšehrad is afforded from the path along the top of the Baroque ramparts, which were built beginning in the mid-seventeenth century. Prague spread out widthways on either side of the life-giving river, which was spanned by a number of bridges.

On a promontory above the left bank, Prague Castle was further developed as a counterpart to Vyšehrad. Since the ninth century, it has been the seat of Bohemian monarchs and, from 1918 to this day, the seat of Czechoslovak and Czech presidents. Around this symbol of Bohemian and then Czech statehood was founded the Castle district (Hradčany) and, below it, the Lesser Town (Malá Strana).

The landmark of the Castle precinct is St Vitus', which became a cathedral when Prague became an archdiocese, in 1344, at the impetus primarily of Charles IV. The present appearance of the cathedral is the result of six centuries of building. Its eastern part, the choir with the chapels, and the Great Tower on the south side were built in the fourteenth century and the beginning of the fifteenth century by the masons' lodges of Matthew of Arras and Peter Parler of Gmünd in Swabia. The tower, however, was not finished until the Renaissance and was remodelled in the eighteenth century. The western part of the cathedral, including the transept, the nave and flanking aisles, and the main façade with the steeples, was finished, in a Neo-Gothic style, only in the nineteenth century, on plans by Josef Mocker. It was completed in 1929, to mark the millennium of the death of St Wenceslas, the principal patron saint of Bohemia. The cathedral silhouette, surrounded by palaces of royals and nobles, forms the instantly recognizable panorama of Prague.

3A, B/ THE VIEWS FROM VYŠEHRAD

The view to the north looking downstream includes the island called Císařská louka (Emperor's Mead) and, further on, Smíchov, which began to develop on the left bank as an industrial district in the mid-eighteenth century. Looking south across the river from the Vyšehrad ramparts, we see the hills of the Vltava valley on the horizon.

Opposite Vyšehrad Rock is the northern tip of Císařská louka. Originally it was not an island but a large low part of the riverbank. Its original name was Královská louka (King's Mead), because of the great celebrations accompanying the coronation of Wenceslas II in 1297. Later, under Habsburg rule, it was renamed Císařská louka. Because it is low lying and frequently in danger of being inundated, nothing was built on this part of the floodplain and, until the end of the nineteenth century, it served the people of Prague as a place of recreation and sport, including horse racing, shooting competitions, and football matches. From 1899 to 1903, part of the mainland was dug away and a modern mooring place for rafts was built and named Francis Joseph I (who, during his visit to Prague in 1907, even came to look at it). The wharves were equipped with three electric hoists to move timber and with industrial spurs for a railway link. It was 1,592 metres long on both banks, that of the mainland and that of the island, and as much as 110 metres wide, and could easily accommodate 200 rafts. After the demise of timber rafting on the Vltava, the rafts were replaced by pleasure craft and the port is today one of the main mooring places in Prague. Various yachting, swimming, and canoeing clubs also have their headquarters and boathouses on the island.

4A, B/ PODOLÍ COVE (PODOLSKÁ ZÁTOKA)

The view from the ramparts down to the river from Vyšehrad Rock returns us to the present. The Podolí port, originally built, from 1869 to 1890, for rafts that moved timber from the Schwarzenberg forests in south Bohemia, was given a protective levee in 1890. After the rafting dock in Smíchov was finished and put into operation, rowing and yachting clubs took over the Podolí port. On the levee stands a wooden building from 1912 (now listed) with a boathouse that belongs to the Český Yacht Klub, together with the clubhouse of Regatta, originally a German rowing club, from the end of the nineteenth century. Other boathouses of sports clubs are on Veslařský ostrov (Rowers' Island), further south.

5A–C/ THE CUBIST HOUSES BELOW VYŠEHRAD

Before the tunnel was built, the road from the centre of Prague to Vyšehrad Rock ended at the house of the ferryman. In order to continue walking south, one could take a ferry around the cliff. Horse-drawn carriages, however, could not get to Podolí except by a long detour.

After the completion of the tunnel, a riverside road was built and new houses were erected along it. The result is an architecturally valuable enclave of modernist houses, whose shapes and ornamentation make inventive use of elements of Cubism. The first from the cliff consists of the three attached single-family houses, nos. 42/6, 47/8, 71/10. This triplex was built in 1912–13, on plans by the architect Josef Chochol. He was also the architect of apartment house no. 70/14, built by F. J. Hodek on the corner of Neklanova and Přemyslova streets. Further building on the embankment was blocked by a row of apartment houses erected in the 1880s and 1890s. The little triangular island of buildings between the Rašínovo nábřeží and the streets Libušina and Vnislavova comprises three single-family houses built in 1912–13. They superbly represent their original owners and the styles of the period: geometricizing Art Nouveau (no. 48/5, designed by Otakar Novotný), Neo-Classicism (no. 50/26, by Emil Králíček), and Cubism (no. 49/3, called Kovařovic House, by Josef Chochol).

THE THREE ATTACHED SINGLE-FAMILY
HOUSES, NOS. 42/6, 47/8, AND 71/10 (1912–13)
The figural ornamentation of the five-sided gable of the
middle house draws on old Czech legends. The architect was
Josef Chochol, a distinctive Czech proponent of Cubism
in building, particularly in the houses concentrated below
Vyšehrad.

THE FAMILY HOUSE AT NO. 49/3
LIBUŠINA ULICE (1912–13)
The main façade of this house by the Prague builder
Bedřich Kovařovic was conceived by the architect Josef
Chochol almost as if it were for an apartment building,
whereas the rear façade (shown in the photograph), with
its projection, corresponds more to the Cubist garden.

6A–C/ THE RAILWAY BRIDGE (ŽELEZNIČNÍ MOST) BELOW VYŠEHRAD

One hundred and forty years ago, Vyšehrad Rock, when seen from the city, seemed to be adorned with the lacework of the iron construction of the railway bridge on the line between (since 1872) Francis Joseph I Station (today, Main Station) and the Western Line Station (today, Smíchov Station). The original upper structure had five trapezoidal bays on five piers, and the bridge had a single track. After thirty years of service it was decided to widen the bridge for a second track and to increase its load-bearing capacity. The rebuilding of the bridge, which took place in a mere three days, from 30 September to 1 October 1901, became one of the legendary engineering feats of contemporary Prague. After new piers were built in the riverbed, scaffolding was erected on one side of the bridge, upon which the new assembled structured was prepared, and on the other side a second scaffolding was erected onto which the old structure was taken down to make room for the new one. The day after the changing of the structures, load testing was carried out, and the day after that the bridge was already in full operation. The bridge stands on two piers. Its upper structure comprises three segmented bays, and it has a footbridge on each side. Regularly maintained, the bridge is still in service today, and though it is listed as a national heritage site, Prague transport planners still have not abandoned the idea of replacing it with a brand new bridge for both rail and motor vehicle transport.

The upper embankment, which forms the bank of Smíchov from the Railway Bridge to Palacký Bridge has, since the second half of the nineteenth century, always been of an industrial and utilitarian character. This is where steamboats of the Prague Steamboat Company were repaired and where the swimming baths and clubhouses of the rowing clubs were moored. They have long been replaced by a botel and other boats working on the river. Down by the river, one has an impressive view of Vyšehrad Rock, the Railway Bridge, and the busy embankment of New Town.

7A, B/ THE CUSTOMS HOUSE AT VÝTOŇ

On the nearby New Town side of the Railway Bridge stands the last building of the once renowned settlement of Podskalí, the Customs House at Výtoň. Beginning in the mid-sixteenth century the house belonged to the New Town council, which operated its own customs office here, collecting customs duties from the rafts coming up from the south by excising (*vytínání* – hence the place name) a certain number of logs. The current appearance of the house is the result of remodelling in the Renaissance style in 1561. On the first floor is a timbered room, open to the public as part of the City of Prague Museum. The ground floor has, for a number of centuries, served as a pub. The sole decoration on the smooth façade of the old building is a square frame above the door, which contains the emblem of New Town in bas-relief.

PODSKALÍ

The old area called Podskalí ran along the riverbank from Výtoň to places of what is today the beginning of Jirásek Bridge. Old Podskalí gradually vanished with the development, first, of the Palacký Embankment (1876–79; today, the north part of the Rašín Embankment), and then of the Vyšehrad Embankment (1904–07; today, the south part of the Rašín Embankment). The individual little groups of Podskalí houses, although cut off from the river, managed to survive until the grading work for new buildings on the embankment plots. The little Podskalí parish church of the Holy Trinity, Gothic at its core, but later remodelled in the Baroque style, still stands in Trojická ulice. Near Výtoň, the Botič stream flows into the Vltava, but is now channelled through pipe.

8A-D/ THE RAŠÍN EMBANKMENT (RAŠÍNOVO NÁBŘEŽÍ) – SOUTH PART

This section, originally called the Vyšehrad Embankment, is among the most modernly conceived embankments in Prague, with a wide lower level, which makes it possible to enjoy a number of recreational activities here. Built from 1904 to 1907, it was technically equipped with a gauging station, which monitors the surface elevation ('stage') and/or volumetric discharge (flow) of the river over time. This particular gauging station is in the form of a Neo-Baroque pavilion with a cupola and a colonnade above two facing sets of steps (not visible in the photo) connecting the upper and the lower level of the embankment. Its technological function is revealed by the large faces of the gauge and the clock.

The façades on the riverside houses between Výtoň and Zítkovy sady (Zítek Park), which were built in 1911–13, constitute a gallery of period styles, from late Art Nouveau and geometrical modernist architecture to Cubism and Neo-Classicism.

House no. 410/32, on the corner of Rašín Embankment and Na Hrobci Street, merits particular attention. It was designed by Alois Dryák, Tomáš Amena, and Quido Bělský. Its sculptural decoration is by Josef Drahoňovský: in rectangular frames between the windows of the mezzanine are depictions of women with cornucopia or just with fruits of the earth. Also meriting attention is the large building,

no. 390/42, erected for the Consolidated Investment Institute (Všeobecný penzijní ústav). It was designed by Jan Kotěra and Josef Zasche in a geometric modernist style that is moving towards quasi-Cubist forms. For house no. 382/60, on the corner of Dřevná ulice, the architect František Roith, too, chose a geometric modernist style.

The Rašín Embankment

(77)

9A, B/ THE PANORAMA WITH EMMAUS ABBEY
(EMAUZY) AND ZÍTEK PARK (ZÍTKOVY SADY)
Above Zítek Park at the end of Palacký Bridge spreads the
panorama of the Benedictine abbey that has two names, Na
Slovanech and Emauzy. It was founded by Charles IV in
1347, and its perimeter has changed three times since then.
The Gothic abbey church of St Mary and St Jerome originally
had a high hipped roof without a steeple. In the second
half of the seventeenth century, the church was remodelled
in the Baroque style by Spanish Benedictines, who were
its occupants, and they gave the church two steeples with
Baroque onion domes. In 1880 the abbey was transferred
to the Benedictines of Beuron (from southern Germany),

who restored the Gothic appearance of the church, giving its steeples sharply pointed spires again. US Air Force bombardment in February 1945 considerably damaged the church, especially the steeples. Passionate debates were then held about its restoration and particularly what style to choose for the restored steeples. The winning design in the architectural competition was by František Maria Černý. It was carried out in 1968, and is probably the boldest, most inventive, and, despite the great contrasts, also the most harmonic design in Prague when it comes to mixing old and new architecture.

On a large piece of land below Emmaus Abbey, in part of what had been Podskalí, a group of ministry buildings was erected from 1924 to 1929 on plans by the architect Bohumil Hübschmann. The result was a great victory for people who loved old Prague, and, by persistent effort, averted the danger of more tall apartment houses being erected on this stretch of the embankment and obscuring the splendid panorama with the abbey.

Amongst the ministries stands a monument by Josef Mařatka. Called *Prague Honouring Her Sons Who Fell for Freedom* (1929–32), it commemorates the soldiers of the Czechoslovak legions in the First World War. Their victorious banner is being crowned by the figure of a woman, an allegory of Prague. In 1940, during the German occupation, the monument was removed by the Nazi authorities, and was not replaced until 1998.

10A–E/ PALACKÝ BRIDGE (PALACKÉHO MOST) AND THE AREA IN FRONT OF IT

The factories in Smíchov, particularly the Ringhoffer Machine Works, needed a stone bridge across which they could move heavy loads into the city, instead of the Francis I Bridge, which was suspended on chains and was never secure, indeed even used to swing a little. Similarly, the detour across Charles Bridge was disadvantageous for them because it prolonged and complicated transport when passing through the towers at each end. Palacký Bridge was built in 1876–78 on plans by the architect Bedřich Münzberger. From the start, each of the four polygonal pier towers was to be surmounted with a sculptural group. And the towers contained toll booths. The sculptural groups, depicting Czech mythological figures, are by Josef Václav Myslbek: *Libuše's Prophesy*, *The Song of Lumír*, *Záboj and Slavoj*, and *Ctirad and Šárka*. They were installed from 1887 to 1897, but were damaged during the US Air Force bombing on 14 February 1945. After their restoration, it was decided to move the sculptures to the park at the top of Vyšehrad. The stone on the faces of the bridge arches are in subtle shades of the Bohemian national colours, red and white.

THE PALACKÝ MONUMENT

Across from the end of the bridge, on the axis, stands
a monument to the patriotic nineteenth-century Czech
historian-politician František Palacký on the square that also
bears his name. By the sculptor Stanislav Sucharda and the
architect Alois Dryák, the monument was the winning design
in a competition held in 1901. It was unveiled in 1912. At
its centre sits Palacký. The groups of figures on each side
symbolize events in Czech history: Habsburg oppression after
the defeat of the Bohemian estates at the Battle of the White
Mountain in 1620 on the left side and the indomitability of
the Czech people on the right. The figure of the woman at the
top, with her left hand raised high, declares the resurrection
of the nation. The figural group at the back of the monument
symbolizes History.

Palacký Bridge

11A, B/ THE RAŠÍN EMBANKMENT
(RAŠÍNOVO NÁBŘEŽÍ) – NORTH PART

The two blocks of houses on the Rašín Embankment between Palacký Square and Jirásek Square were built from 1889 to 1905. The more southerly block is earlier and its Neo-Renaissance architecture is an example of a common type of building erected in many other Prague locations during the boom. The northern block, more inventive, comprises Neo-Renaissance and early Art Nouveau buildings. Two identical buildings, nos. 1980/70 and 2000/78, were constructed here, on his own design, by the developer Vácslav Havel, in 1904–05. Havel and his family lived in one of them, and his grandson, Václav Havel, also lived here before he became President of Czechoslovakia in December 1989.

The twelve-metre-wide lower level of the embankment below Palacký Bridge was not added to the embankment wall (1876–79) until 1905. It was intended as a practical measure for people on excursions, who had previously boarded Prague steamboats from this wharf by first descending steep iron steps. This section of the embankment still functions as a wharf, and from here one can admire the earliest paddle steamboats of the Prague fleet still in operation: the *Vyšehrad*, built in 1938, and the *Vltava*, built in 1940 – two floating heritage monuments.

In the years when Václav Havel was still a dissident, he and his friends often used to meet in the Vltava restaurant, which at the time was called Paroplavba (Steam Navigation). This wooden building on the lower level of the embankment by the Palacký Bridge was established as a family-run business in 1945, but was nationalized after the Communist takeover in early 1948. After the collapse of the Communist régime in late 1989, it was eventually returned to the original restaurateur. In 1995 it was listed as a national monument.

12A–C/ JIRÁSEK BRIDGE (JIRÁSKŮV MOST)

Built in 1929–32, Jirásek Bridge, linking New Town at the extension of Resslova ulice (Ressel Street) with Smíchov, is the most recent of the bridges in the centre of Prague. It is by the architect Vlastislav Hofman, who aimed to design a visually light structure that would easily and elegantly hover over the surface of the water. In the little park at the end of the bridge a monument to the writer Alois Jirásek was erected in 1960. The sculptor was Karel Pokorný; the architect was Jaroslav Fragner.

THE DANCING HOUSE (TANČÍCÍ DŮM)

On the vacant plot on the corner of Jirásek Square and the Rašín Embankment, whose original building was destroyed by US Air Force bombing on 14 February 1945, an iconic work of modern Prague architecture was erected from 1992 to 1996. Called the Dancing House or, alternatively, Ginger and Fred, its tower corners suggest a man dancing with a woman whose skirt is billowing out. The design of the inventive shape is by the Canadian-born American architect Frank O. Gehry and the Czech architect of Croatian origin Vlado Milunić. When it was going up, the building met with mixed reactions, because it was the first of this type of world architecture to enter the traditional Prague environment. As it later turned out, however, the contrast with the other embankment houses, which tend to be uniform in height and style, is irrefutably refreshing.

Jirásek Bridge

13A, B/ THE MASARYK EMBANKMENT
(MASARYKOVO NÁBŘEŽÍ)

Originally named after the politician František Ladislav
Rieger, the Masaryk Embankment was built in a place once
called Vojtěšská čtvrť (the Adalbert Quarter), named after
the little parish church of St Adalbert (Vojtěch) in nearby
Vojtěšská ulice. The riverbank was covered with mills and
workshops of various trades. As the only part of New Town
that was continuously under threat from floods, it was
included in the Prague slum clearance, which mainly affected
the former Jewish quarter, called Josefov (Josefstadt), and
parts of Old Town. The houses and mills here were bought
up by City Hall and then, in 1903–5, were demolished. In
their place, a section of embankment was built with a road
and new apartment buildings. Perhaps because of its nearness
to the National Theatre and its view of Prague Castle, the
developers decided to build luxurious and yet affordable flats,
and sought to out do each other in the decorativeness and
showiness of these houses. The southernmost block between
Jiráskovo náměstí and Myslíkova ulice comprises richly
ornamented Neo-Baroque and Neo-Gothic houses built in
1906–7. This is true also of the other blocks of embankment
houses that were built in 1904–5 in various combinations of
revival styles and also Art Nouveau. Amongst them, house
no. 248/16 merits particular mention. It was built for the
Prague Hlahol Choir (Pražský zpěvácký spolek Hlahol), and
consequently includes a concert hall. This important work of
Art Nouveau architecture, designed by Josef Fanta, is covered
with artistic ornamentation, inside and out. The picture in
the gable, by K. L. Klusáček, is painted on ceramic tiles, and
is an allegory of Music. The sculpture ornamentation on the
façade is by Josef Pekárek, the other ornamentation is by
Karel Mottl, and the sgraffito is again by Klusáček.

The Masaryk Embankment

14A, B/ THE ŠÍTKA WATER TOWER
(ŠÍTKOVSKÁ VODÁRENSKÁ VĚŽ)
From the Masaryk Embankment one can take a little
footbridge to the nearby Slovanský ostrov (Slav Island).
The Šítka Water Tower, bearing the name of the owner
of mills that originally stood nearby, is a landmark of the
whole area. It supplied water from the Vltava to upper New
Town. The predecessors of today's tower were destroyed
by fire. The current tower was built from 1588 to 1591, and
its characteristic onion-dome roof dates from repairs made
in 1651 after being damaged during the Thirty Years' War
(which ended in 1648). After the waterworks went out of
operation in 1880, the tower was threatened with demolition.

THE MÁNES SOCIETY OF ARTISTS

The Mánes Society of Artists (Spolek výtvarných umělců
Mánes) acquired the Šítka Mills and, in their place, from
1928 to 1930, built a Functionalist building, no. 250/1,
with an exhibition hall and spaces for the society's work
and other activities. Together with the former water tower,
it creates an imposing whole. The building stands partly
over an arm of the Vltava between Slovanský ostrov (Slav
Island) and the embankment and partly on the island itself.
This architecturally valuable building was designed with
extraordinary sensitivity by Otakar Novotný.

15A, B/ SLAV ISLAND (SLOVANSKÝ OSTROV)

This island resulted from the consolidation of the remainder of flood deposits after the great flood of 1784. Later it began to be used for recreation, baths, and trade. A dyeworks (*barvírna*) for fabrics was located here, hence its original name, Barvířský ostrov or, popularly, Barvířka. In 1838, in honour of the future monarch Francis Joseph I's mother, it was renamed Sophie Island, popularly known in Czech as Žofín. Beginning in 1836, there was a single-storey building here with a restaurant and a hall for exhibitions, concerts, dances, and balls. On the east side of the island, along an arm of the Vltava, several buildings were erected for a bathing facility. In 1884, the island was purchased by the town council, and the municipal building authorities then grandly remodelled the community centre in a Neo-Renaissance style. Today, after many restorations, it still serves its original purpose. Until the Municipal House (Obecní dům) was built on the other side of town, Žofín was the centre of Prague social life. The buildings of the baths were torn down in 1928, and today part of the promenade on the island runs through land on which they once stood. Slovanský ostrov will probably remain the most visited Prague island. A number of restaurants on pontoons and boat hire companies attract people who want to be close to the river without leaving the city.

A MONUMENT TO BOŽENA NĚMCOVÁ

In the park in front of the community centre, a monument was raised, in 1955, to Božena Němcová, a nineteenth-century Czech writer mostly of prose fiction. By the sculptor Karel Pokorný and the architect Jaroslav Fragner, the monument commemorates Božena Němcová's participation in the balls that Czech patriots used to organize at Žofín in the 1840s.

(97)

16A, B/ THE PETRŽILKA WATER TOWER AND WEIR (PETRŽILKOVSKÁ VODÁRENSKÁ VĚŽ AND PETRŽILKOVSKÝ JEZ)

Crossing Jirásek Bridge from the right to the left bank of the Vltava affords views of Slovanský ostrov, the water tower, the building of the Mánes Art Society from the river side, and the historic Prague weirs. The shape of the Petržilka Weir has changed greatly over the years; there used to be a whole system of interlinked weirs here, which channelled water to several groups of mills on the right and the left bank. With a straight shape that breaks on an angle and with a raft sluice in the middle of the river, the weir was built in connection with the regulation of the channels and the building of the lock by the riverbank in Smíchov in the 1910s.

From the bridge one also has a good view of another Renaissance water tower in Prague, called both the Malostranská věž (the Lesser Town Water Tower) and the Petržilkovská věž, after the name of the island it stands on. It was erected in 1561–2 on the site of an earlier wooden tower, and, until 1886, it supplied water to the Lesser Town. The tower stands on the remains of what was originally Petržilka Island, which was cleaned up as part of the construction of the Smíchov lock. Vessels enter it from above the weir just by the tower.

On the left bank, the Jirásek Bridge leads into, and off of, the centre of the Janáček Embankment, which is divided here by Dienzenhoferovy sady (Dienzenhofer Park). The park is named after a great Baroque architect, whose summer house stood on the riverbank here until the bridge was built. Before the row of trees along the street became so tall, the façades of the newly built houses used to be clearly visible from many sides, as too were the houses on the embankment across the river. Their luxuriousness was intended as a grand statement about their owner and the social status of the residents. The façades are textbook examples of the aesthetics of the period and how it developed.

From Jirásek Bridge heading south to Palacký Bridge, three blocks of houses were built from 1907 to 1910. One's attention is drawn particularly to three late Art Nouveau houses: no. 84/9, designed by Emil Dufek, with sculptural ornamentation by Jindřich Čapek, wooden ornamentation, and a large half-timbered gable; house no. 86/7, designed by Ladislav Čapek, with sculptural ornamentation by Josef Drahoňovský; and house no. 85/5, by Richard Klenka z Vlastimilu, with ornamental panels between the windows.

The part of the embankment north of Jirásek Bridge as far as the Bridge of the Legions comprises six blocks of houses, which were built gradually from 1876 to 1905; the further south they are, the later these houses date from. While moving from south to north one should keep an eye out for the corner house, no. 1055/21, designed by Ferdinand Šamonil, from 1903, with bands of ornamentation based on drawings by Mikoláš Aleš on a theme from Chodsko, south Bohemia. The corner house, no. 729/31, by the architect Jan Zeyer, was built in 1891 in the style of the Czech Neo-Renaissance, and is decorated with painted scenes of Princess Libuše's prophesy and with figures of queens of Bohemia; the decoration has its counterpart on another corner house, no. 91/35, with full-length portraits of kings of Bohemia. The last three blocks on the embankment are Neo-Renaissance and far more subtle; they were built by private investors in the short period from 1876 to 1880, similarly to the stretch of the Ferdinand Embankment (today the Janáček Embankment).

THE SMÍCHOV LOCK

Because of the frequency of private tourist boats sailing through it, the Smíchov lock, built between the Janáček Embankment and Dětský ostrov (Children's Island) from 1913–1921, is the busiest lock on the Vltava. It has two chambers, one after the other, with a total length of 175 metres. Boats sailing from the south return to the main watercourse through the canal, more than 400 metres long, emerging below the Old Town Weir (Staroměstký jez) by Charles Bridge, thus surmounting the levels of two weirs.

The Janáček Embankment

18/ CHILDREN'S ISLAND (DĚTSKÝ OSTROV)

This long island, bordered by the riverbank at Smíchov between Jirásek Bridge and the Bridge of the Legions, has had several names over the years, depending on who owned it. In the nineteenth century it was called Židovský ostrov (Jews' Island), because it belonged to the Porges von Portheim family, the Jewish owners of the nearby factories for chintz (printed calico) or fancy cotton, who operated a bleachery here. Since the 1960s, it has been called Dětský ostrov (Children's Island), because several new sports grounds and playgrounds were built here at that time.

The island is connected to the mainland by a small bridge built on the piers of a bridge planned in the 1920s to run from below the water tower at the south entrance to the lock, but was ultimately never built.

A good view of the northern tip of Dětský ostrov, where the lock ends and the canal begins, is afforded from the Bridge of the Legions. The architectural design of the island is particularly interesting. From the tip of the island, which has a small stone circular colonnade, steps lead down to the foot of a pylon surmounted by a three-metre high woman in bronze, an allegory of the Vltava. Below her, on the four sides of the square pylon, are high-relief sculptures depicting the four tributaries of the Vltava: the Otava, the Lužnice, the Sázava, and the Berounka rivers. The monument is the work of the sculptor Josef Pekárek. On All Soul's Day, a memorial service, traditionally organized by the Vltavan Society, is held here at the statue for all those who drowned in the river during the year.

19/ THE LESSER TOWN EMBANKMENT
(MALOSTRANSKÉ NÁBŘEŽÍ)
One can enter the island of Kampa from the Bridge of
the Legions by crossing a short stretch of the Lesser
Town Embankment which follows on from the Janáček
Embankment. This section was nameless until 1905. In
the place of a bastion on the fortifications, a block of
Neo-Renaissance apartment houses was built from 1887
to 1892 by Jindřich (Heinrich) Jechenthal.

20A, B/ SHARPSHOOTER ISLAND (STŘELECKÝ OSTROV)

This island, easily accessible from the Bridge of the Legions, was known since the Middle Ages as a place for archers and crossbowmen to practice and compete. In the nineteenth century it was used by the Prague Sharpshooters Corps, a volunteer civil guard, whose task was to protect the town in the event of foreign invasion, but also to participate in numerous parades and celebrations in their handsome uniforms. From the Middle Ages on, shooting at wooden targets became a very popular pastime amongst the people of Prague. At Pentecost it was called 'Shooting at the Bird', and the winner was proclaimed the 'Bird King'. The island was registered as a part of Old Town, which used to lend it to the sharpshooters. When, in 1810, the shooting range, which was made of wood, burnt down, it was decided to erect a building of stone in its place. Thus, in 1812, a Neo-Classical building with a restaurant and community hall was built on plans by the architect Josef Klement Zobel. It is still here today. An interesting feature of the building is the vast passage through the middle of the ground floor, enabling flood waters to pass through it, thus leaving the building unshaken. The people of Prague used this island much as they used Žofín. In the community centre, dances were held and, later, films were shown. A open-air restaurant was built here for summer excursions, and people came here to ice skate in winter. In 1934–36 a restaurant terrace with a splendid view was added on to the building.

The first Sokol meet was organized on Střelecký ostrov in 1882, with the participation of the founder of this physical-training association, Miroslav Tyrš. And in 1890 the first May Day (or International Workers' Day) celebration ever held in Bohemia took place here. In 2010–13 the island was relandscaped.

Sharpshooter Island – the Bridge of the Legions

21A, B/ THE BRIDGE OF THE LEGIONS (MOST LEGIÍ)

The Bridge of the Legions was called the Francis I Bridge until after the First World War, when it was renamed in honour of the legions formed in 1917 by Czech and Slovak soldiers who had deserted from the Austrian Army. This stone bridge was built from 1899 to 1901 to replace the chain bridge that was no longer suitable (indeed, its swinging to and fro used to make people walking across it uneasy). The new bridge was designed in a revival style by the architect Antonín Balšánek. From the bridge one is afforded a view of the beginning of the street between New Town and Old Town, which today is called Národní třída (National Avenue). On its right corner, in New Town, stands the monumental National Theatre.

22A, B/ THE NATIONAL THEATRE
(NÁRODNÍ DIVADLO)

The construction of this Czech sanctuary of the muses was in itself dramatic. It took thirty years from the formulation of the intention to make a national theatre until it was finally opened. On the plot of land by the river, which became available after the demolition of the municipal salthouse of New Town, a Provisional Theatre was first built, in 1862, so that Czech theatre productions could begin without further delay. The winner of the architectural competition for its future building, held in 1866, was Josef Zítek, whose design was in the style of the Italian Renaissance with a roof like an upside-down ship's hull. The next year, during the Feast of St John Nepomucene, on 16 May, the foundation stone was laid. Because construction was financed by nation-wide fundraising, the work, with lavish artistic decoration of the interior, went slowly. In June 1881, the theatre was officially opened, but an act of carelessness by the workers led to the building being burnt to the ground on 12 August of that year. The tragedy, which was profoundly felt throughout the nation, provided the impetus to begin feverish new fundraising activity, and thanks to it the theatre could be rebuilt within two years. Because of disputes with the theatre management, Zítek no longer participated in the rebuilding; his task was taken over by his close colleague Josef Schulz. The theatre was finally opened in 1883.

To mark its hundredth anniversary the theatre underwent a complete renovation from 1977 to 1983, and new buildings were added on, including the Nová scéna (New Stage) by the architect Karel Prager.

23A, B/ THE SMETANA EMBANKMENT (SMETANOVO NÁBŘEŽÍ)

Work began on the first Prague embankment, originally called Františkovo nábřeží (after the Emperor Francis I), in 1841, immediately after the completion of the nearby chain bridge over Střelecký ostrov, and finished in 1845.

The embankment project, financed from Bohemian public funds, was not limited only to erecting an embankment wall. It also included the urban plan for the houses to be built on it. This is where a city promenade with a view of Prague Castle was to be built. The houses, designed by the architect Bernhard Grueber, of a maximum height of three storeys, were planned for three blocks. The middle block receded to make a small square with a monument. In the spirit of this plan, the late Neo-Classicist houses nos. 334/4, 995/6, 331/8, 324/10, and 325/12 were built here from 1846 to 1854. On the corner of Národní třída was built the Neo-Renaissance Lažanský House, no. 1012/2, by Ignác Vojtěch Ullmann, from 1861 to 1863. Since 1884, it has been home to one of the most famous Prague cafés, the Slavia.

On the northern edge of the row of houses, where the embankment meets the street Karolíny Světlé, is a house of striking colour and form: with two house numbers, 329/8 and 330/16, it has a corner tower reminiscent of the Northern Renaissance. The building, known by the name of the café inside it, the Bellevue, was designed by Konstantin Mráček, and was built from 1893 to 1897.

A monument to Francis I, the Emperor of Austria, was built from 1845 to 1850 in the little park amongst the houses. Called *The Homage of the Bohemian Estates*, it is a fountain with a Gothic pinnacle designed by Josef Kranner, hence its being popularly known as the Kranner Fountain. The sculptural works are by Josef Max. The central point of the monument is a bronze equestrian statute of the monarch, below which stand allegorical figures of the then sixteen regions of Bohemia, with Prague at the head. When Austria-Hungary was broken apart and the Czechoslovak Republic was declared in late 1918, the statue of the emperor was removed from the pedestal and was deposited in the Lapidarium of the National Museum. A copy was returned to the monument in 2003.

24/ THE OLD TOWN MILLS AND WATER TOWER (STAROMĚSTSKÉ MLÝNY AND STAROMĚSTSKÁ VĚŽ)

The Old Town Mills are the only buildings of their kind to have been preserved on the Vltava. In the second half of the nineteenth century there were still eight groups of buildings that had originally been mills and similarly projected into the river on the banks of Old Town and New Town. The Old Town Mills were built before 1347 (the date of the first record of them). Their appearance changed with rebuilding after frequent fires. They were given their current appearance after the great fires of 1848 and 1878. The restored buildings were then given façades in the romanticizing styles of the Neo-Gothic and Neo-Renaissance. A good example is the corner building, no. 198/39, called Karlovy lázně (the Charles Baths), which was built as a mill in 1879, but was later used as public baths. In the 1970s, some of the mill buildings, particularly the substructure of the water tower, were thoroughly restored from the inside. During this work, their façades, decorated in revival styles, were respectfully preserved, and, above the mill 'lagoon', the façades on the north side, where the milling had been done, were restored with plain surfaces.

The former Old Town waterworks, which stands over the weir at the edge of the group, was built from 1882 to 1884 in a Neo-Renaissance style on plans by Antonín Wiehl. The surfaces between the windows on the attic storey are lavishly decorated with sgraffito depicting battles between the people of Prague and the Swedish army in 1648, the last clashes of the Thirty Years' War, made after cartoons by František Ženíšek and Mikoláš Aleš. In 1936, the Bedřich Smetana Museum was opened in the building. A bronze monument to the composer, by Josef Malejovský, was unveiled on an observation deck below the building in 1984. Originally, only a wooden gangway led round the mills to the waterworks. When a new waterworks was built, the gangway was reinforced, which has, since 1885, been called Novotného lávka (Novotný Footbridge) in honour of the well-known milling family that operated mills here for several generations.

The most prominent building of the Old Town Mills is the water tower, whose wooden predecessor had stood here since at least 1341. It was replaced, at the latest in 1489, by a Late Gothic stone structure, and rebuilt in a Renaissance style in 1576–7. After the fire of 1848, the top stage of the tower was remodelled in a Neo-Gothic style and given a pseudo-Gothic pyramid roof.

25A, B/ KNIGHTS OF THE CROSS SQUARE (KŘIŽOVNICKÉ NÁMĚSTÍ)

Křižovnické náměstí, two sides of which are formed by the monumental façades of St Francis of Assisi Church (svatého Františka Serafínského) and St Saviour's Church (Nejsvětějšího Salvátora) and the third side by the Old Town Bridge Tower with the gate to Charles Bridge, is considered one of the most stunning outdoor spaces in Prague.

The bronze monument to Charles IV, by Ernst Julius Hähnel, was meant to be unveiled in April 1848 to mark the 500th anniversary of the founding of Prague University. But because of revolutionary activity, the celebration was postponed and the monument was not erected until 1851. Below the figure of the monarch are allegorical depictions of the four university faculties – theology, medicine, law, and the arts.

THE CHURCH OF ST SAVIOUR (KOSTEL NEJSVĚTĚJŠÍHO SALVÁTORA)

The church, occupying the east side of the square, is part of the Clementinum, which was as a Jesuit collegium and is the second largest historic complex in Prague. After the reforms of the Emperor Joseph II (*reg.* 1765–90), this important educational institution was transformed into a library, and has remained one ever since. Today, it is the National Library of the Czech Republic. The Church of St Saviour is among the oldest parts of the complex. Plans to build it were already being made in 1578, during the Renaissance, but its façade, with the magisterial Early Baroque portico, was not made until after 1655, on plans by Carlo Lurago, with the participation of the Bohemian sculptor Johann Georg (Jan Jiří) Bendl. His statues of Christ the Saviour and the Blessed Virgin Mary hold the most important place in the architectural composition of the main façade, with a balcony over the entrance porch. The whole Clementinum was finished in the 1720s.

THE CHURCH OF ST FRANCIS OF ASSISI (KOSTEL SV. FRANTIŠKA SERAFÍNSKÉHO)

The church of the Order of the Knights of the Cross is a work of Early Baroque architecture. It was built from 1679 to 1685, on plans by the French-born architect Jean-Baptiste Mathey. Above the ornately decorated façade of the church rises the distinctive drum and cupola. The monastery and hospital of the Knights of the Cross with the Red Star were founded on the bank of the Vltava at the Old Town end of Charles Bridge in 1252, on the initiative of Agnes of Bohemia. Indeed, in 1233 she even founded this purely Bohemian Order. After being damaged during the Swedish siege of Prague in 1648, the convent of the monastery was rebuilt in 1661–3. Later, for the generalate, a wing was built over the river. Best seen from Charles Bridge, it stands above the first arch of what remains of the Romanesque Judith Bridge, and the mass of the generalate also conceals its Romanesque tower. From 1909 to 1912, the monastery buildings, except for the generalate and the church, were demolished, and a Neo-Baroque structure designed by Josef Sakař was built in their place.

THE OLD TOWN BRIDGE TOWER
(STAROMĚSTSKÁ MOSTECKÁ VĚŽ)

The Gothic bridge tower, from the second half of the
fourteenth century, is the work of the master mason of
St Vitus' Cathedral, Peter Parler. Walking through or by
it, one would hardly realize that it was built not on the
riverbank but on the first pier of the bridge. The sculptural
decoration on the east side of the tower, facing the square,
is full of the symbolism that Charles IV's period loved. It
is hierarchically divided into individual spheres from the
terrestrial, symbolized by small genre scenes, to the celestial,
with the figures of two patron saints of Bohemia, Adalbert
(Vojtěch) and Sigismund (Zikmund). In the middle field of
the celestial or monarchical sphere, above the top of the gate,
are Charles IV and his son Wenceslas IV enthroned; depicted
between them is Charles Bridge, and above it is Vitus, the
patron saint of the bridge. The western façade of the tower
was badly damaged by Swedish artillery fire in 1648, but
from the historic scenes, particularly the morbid depiction of
the heads of twelve of the twenty-seven executed Bohemian
gentlemen exhibited on the tower gallery in 1621, it is clear
that it too was richly decorated.

Not named after its founder, Charles IV, until about 1870, it was originally called Stone Bridge and also Prague Bridge. It was built, between 1357 and about 1402, of sandstone ashlars. It is 516 metres long and was originally 9.5 metres wide. It stands on seventeen piers, with sixteen arches. Its founding has traditionally been linked with the magic series of odd numbers 1–3–5–7–9–7–5–3–1, allegedly meant to provide it with astrological protection: following the numbers of the year 1357 comes the ninth day of the seventh month and then the fifth hour and the thirty-first minute.

Today it is hard to imagine Charles Bridge without its Baroque sculptural ornamentation, but it has not always looked this way. On its road bed once stood only a stone column shrine and opposite it, where a Calvary now stands, there was a cross with a depiction of the body of Christ. The cross was restored several times, and the figures of Our Lady of Sorrows and St John the Evangelist were added to it. The cross that is there now was erected in 1657. The gilt inscription in Hebrew, from 1695, was paid for by a fine given to a certain Prague Jew because he had allegedly mocked the cross.

Among the earliest stone sculptures on the bridge is the *Pietà* by Johann Brokoff from 1695, which took the place of the column shrine. The other stone sculptures and sculptural groups of saints, by the best Baroque sculptors in Bohemia, like Ferdinand Maximilian Brokoff and his father Johann Brokoff, Mathias Wenzel Jäckel, and, especially, Matthias Bernhard Braun, were all installed on the bridge by 1714. The composition of the sculptures later changed after the floods of 1784 and 1890 and military conflicts. The Baroque sandstone sculptural groups have suffered by exposure to the elements and vandalism, and are gradually being replaced with copies. The originals, however, can be viewed in the Lapidarium of the National Museum at the Exhibition Grounds (Výstaviště) and in Gorlice Hall at Vyšehrad.

For a full list of the statues and a diagram, see pp. 184–87.

ST JOHN NEPOMUCENE

The first statue of John Nepomucene (Jan z Nepomuku) was made of wood, and was placed on the bridge in about 1650. In 1683 it was replaced by a cast-bronze masterpiece, the work of Johann Brokoff, which stands on the bridge to this day. This portrait of a major Bohemian saint – the patron saint of bridges and of people whose work is linked with water, and a heavenly protector against floods – became an iconographic model for his many other portrayals throughout central Europe. Inlaid in the top of the parapet, roughly midway across the bridge, is a little bronze cross, and above it a copy of a Baroque grille with a relief sculpture of St John Nepomucene, marking what is allegedly the place from which, as vicar general, he was hurled into the river. The spot attracts millions of tourists because of the legend that whoever puts his or her hand on the sculpture will have his or her wishes fulfilled.

ST LUDMILA

The sculptural group depicts the Přemyslid princess Ludmila (c.860–921), who became a patron saint of Bohemia, and her young grandson Wenceslas (c.907–935). It was made by Matthias Bernhard Braun in 1720, and was moved from the ramp of Prague Castle to the bridge after a statue of St Wenceslas, by Ottavio Mosto, was swept into the Vltava in the flood of 1784.

BRUNCVÍK

On the last pier in the riverbed on the Lesser Town side of the river stands a statue of the legendary knight Bruncvík (a figure possibly derived from Henry the Lion, the Count of Brunswick, or Roland, Charlemagne's paladin, an emblem of borough rights throughout the Holy Roman Empire). Wearing a suit of armour and holding his sword in his right hand, and resting his left hand on top of his shield bearing the Old Town coat of arms, he is meant to show that Charles Bridge is part of Old Town. The statue was erected here in the early sixteenth century, but was badly damaged in 1648 by artillery fire in battles with Swedish troops. In 1884, the damaged sculpture, allegedly of alabaster, was replaced by a sandstone copy roughly corresponding to the original.

27/ THE LESSER TOWN END OF CHARLES BRIDGE

When walking across Charles Bridge to Lesser Town (Malá Strana), it is clear that almost one third of the bridge stands above dry land. Approaching Lesser Town, one is welcomed by the two bridge towers, whose different appearances immediately suggest their different origins. The one on the left bank was the tower of the Romanesque Judith Bridge, from before 1172. Its façade, gables, and roof, however, are Renaissance, from 1591. On the wall of this tower, facing the bridge, though concealed by the later little house, no. 56/1, of the Old Town customs office, there remains preserved a large Romanesque relief sculpture, which depicts a still unidentified action taking placed between two figures, one seated (perhaps on a throne), the other kneeling. This smaller tower, which is called the Judith Tower, has, since 1927, been the headquarters of the Klub Za starou Prahu (Society for the Preservation of Old Prague). The larger tower was erected after 1400, in connection with the building of Charles Bridge. Although richly decorated with Gothic stone elements, it has no figural decoration.

28A–E/ KAMPA

The island called Kampa was created on the left side of the Vltava by alluvial deposits and partly also by the great fire in Lesser Town in 1541, when rubble from the demolished buildings was dumped here. Kampa acquired the character of an island thanks to an arm of the Vltava, called Čertovka (the Devil's Mill Race), which has been adapted for a series of mills. Today, one can easily walk through the island as a park, but originally it was divided amongst the adjacent noble houses of the Nostitz, Michna, and Lichtenstein families, the parts serving as their private gardens. Through the middle of the island ran a path between high garden walls, resembling a narrow mountain pass, which at least enabled one to walk from south to north or vice versa. One can reach Kampa from Charles Bridge by descending one of two facing flights of steps that were built in the 1840s. The island was made into a public park only after the Second World War.

At Čertovka there are two mills with well-preserved mill wheels: near Charles Bridge is the Velkopřevorský mlýn (Grand Prior's Mill), generally believed to date from the thirteenth century, and on the south part of the island is a mill called the Huť (Lodge), now a café.

LICHTENSTEIN HOUSE
(LICHTENŠTEJNSKÝ PALÁC)

This grand house and its garden were built on the banks of
Kampa in 1697–8 for the Kaiserstein (Kaiserštejn) family. The
architect was probably Giovanni Battista Alliprandi. After
several changes in ownership, it has been called Lichtenstein
House since 1831 when the Lichtenstein family bought it.
Its current appearance is the result of Late Neo-Classical
remodelling after 1864, when it was the property of the
Odkolek family, the owners of the neighbouring flour mill.

ON KAMPA

Kampa is so picturesque largely because of its historic houses, concentrated around the square that was renowned for its pottery fairs. Many of these houses have their own colourful stories, which are also hinted at by their ancient house signs.

Towards the west, Petřín Hill rises up to a height of 327 metres in the middle of Prague behind Kampa. The observation tower at the top of the hill is an approximate copy of the Eiffel Tower in Paris, one fifth its size. Petřín Hill, which seems like one big park, is a popular place for the people of Prague and other visitors to take walks, and is among the most famous landmarks of the city.

THE SOVA MILLS (SOVOVY MLÝNY)

Mills were built on the banks of Kampa too. Water was
supplied by the Old Town Weir. The core of the Renaissance
building of the Sova Mills dates from 1589. It is named after
its owner at that time, the miller Václav Sova z Liboslav,
and has been remodelled often since then, most strikingly
after it became the property of the miller and industrialist
František Odkolek in the mid-nineteenth century – which is
why it sometimes also called Odkolek Mills. The building
was remodelled after 1867 in the Romantic Neo-Gothic style.
Since the building was damaged by fire in 1896 and was
left derelict for quite some time, the city of Prague bought
it, repaired it, and built workshops here. Today, the former
mill, adapted after 2000, houses the Museum Kampa with its
collection of modern art.

29A–D/ PRAGUE VENICE
(PRAŽSKÉ BENÁTKY)

The Čertovka (Devil's Mill Race) flows under
Charles Bridge towards the Vltava. The
riverbank here is densely lined with the historic
houses along the street U Lužického semináře
(By the Lusatian Seminary), and their back
sides rise out of the water like the houses on the
canals of Venice.

THE HERGET BRICKYARD
(HERGETOVA CIHELNA)

An important lower part of the typical panorama of Prague,
the riverbank where the Čertovka flows into the Vltava has
almost completely retained its original historic appearance.
The building of the last riverside brickyard in Prague still
stands preserved on the rounded headland. The Herget
Brickyard, with its entrance on Cihelná ulice, was built after
1780. By remodelling and additions, a house for the owner of
the brickyard and his family was built here in a Neo-Classical
style. Despite further remodelling in the nineteenth and
twentieth centuries, the brickyard, with its mansard roof and
turret, when seen from the riverside at Old Town, continues
to look as it did when depicted in old topographically
accurate cityscape prints and paintings.

Behind the brickyard is the only natural river landing
in the historic centre of the city. It is popular amongst
families with children as a place to observe and feed water
fowl, particularly swans. This picturesque corner between
the riverbank and the small historic buildings, which were
originally part of the medieval riverside settlement called
Rybáře (The Fishermen's Place), is today popular with
tourists.

30/ THE ALEŠ EMBANKMENT (ALŠOVO NÁBŘEŽÍ)

The riverbank of the Old Town north of the Knights of the Cross monastery was once a place for doing traditional crafts, and included a tannery, a wash house, a bleachery, and timber yards. Formerly called the Crown Prince Rudolph Embankment, the Aleš Embankment was built here in 1875–6 and was subsequently developed with a complex of Neo-Renaissance school buildings.

Mánes Bridge

(143)

31A–D/ MÁNES BRIDGE (MÁNESŮV MOST)

This bridge, made mostly of reinforced concrete but also stone, links Lesser Town with Old Town at the Rudolfinum. It was built from 1911 to 1914 to take the place of the chain bridge called the Rudolph Footbridge. The modernist new bridge with Cubist motifs was designed by the architect Mečislav Petrů. The ornamentation in sculptural relief, by František Bílek, Josef Mařatka, and Jan Štursa, can be seen only from a boat.

Originally named after the Archduke Franz Ferdinand, it was rechristened Mánes Bridge in 1920, after the great Czech painter Josef Mánes, a bronze statue of whom was placed, in 1951, in the little park between the river and the Rudolfinum on the Old Town end of the bridge. The Mánes monument was made in 1940 by the sculptor Bohumil Kafka.

KLÁROV

The Lesser Town end of Mánes Bridge is called Klárov, after Alois Klar, the founder of the nearby Klar Institute for the Blind in house no. 131/3. This austere, large, Neo-Classical building was erected from 1836 to 1844 and in 1884–5. The park at Klárov was made after demolishing army bakeries and storehouses in 1917. Today the east side of the park is bordered by an overly high wall of apartment houses erected to line the continuation of the street coming off the chain footbridge built in 1868–9 to link Klárov with Old Town. Mánes Bridge, however, was planned in a slightly shifted direction, and the apartment houses thus inadvertently ended up off this busy street. To make room for the new bridge and to allow it to end in Lesser Town, most of the small, basically medieval houses of the old Rybáře settlement were demolished.

In the background of the photo on the right one can see the steeple and dome of the Baroque church of St Nicholas (chrám sv. Mikuláše) in Lesser Town and the slender pointed spire of the monastery church of St Thomas. On the left in the background, on the slopes of Petřín Hill, stands an observation tower, built in 1891 as a smaller version of the Eiffel Tower.

The photo on the lower right shows the Klar Institute for the Blind and Charles Bridge behind it.

(145)

(146)

32A, B/ THE STRAKA ACADEMY (STRAKOVA AKADEMIE) – THE OFFICE OF THE GOVERNMENT
On the left bank of the Vltava, north of Mánes Bridge, between the Kosárek Embankment and the Edvard Beneš Embankment, is the distinctive Straka Academy. On this large pieces of land, the Jesuit Collegium, based at the Clementinum, once had a garden and farm buildings. After the pope suppressed the Jesuit Order in 1773, the land served as a dyeworks and bleachery, and the buildings served as a restaurant and dance hall. The former garden was purchased sometime before 1890 by the foundation that Count Jan Petr Straka z Nedabylic established at the beginning of the eighteenth century. Foundation bursaries paid for the education of sons from impoverished noble families. The imposing building of the Straka Academy was erected from 1891 to 1896 in a Neo-Baroque style on plans by the architect Václav Roštlapil and with sculptural decoration by Josef Mauder. The grand building used to have its own swimming pool, gymnasium, hospital, and everything else in fact that a young nobleman required for his proper development. It did not, however, serve its original purpose for long. During the First World War a Red Cross hospital was set up here, and after 1918 the building was used for offices of the newly established Czechoslovak Republic and other institutions. Since the Second World War, thanks to its prestigious location and grand appearance, the building has housed the Office of the Government.

THE PUBLIC SWIMMING POOL
(OBČANSKÁ PLOVÁRNA)
Also on the riverbank below Letná Park stands the low Neo-Classical pavilion of the Public Swimming Pool, built in 1840. The actual swimming place was chained to a floating wooden structure in the river. It continued to operate until 1989. At present the City of Prague rents out the pavilion and garden to a restaurant.

33A–C/ JAN PALACH SQUARE
(NÁMĚSTÍ JANA PALACHA)

The square was formed in the nineteenth and twentieth centuries solely by the important public buildings that were erected around it. Originally there were timber yards here and a place to exercise horses in summer, hence its original name, Rejdiště, that is, a playground, a place for animals to exercise, or a den of thieves.

Entering the square from Mánes Bridge, one sees a complex of Neo-Renaissance school buildings on the right, which were erected from 1879 to 1885 on plans by Josef Srdínko, František Schmoranz, Jr, and Jan Machytka. The foremost building of this block, facing the square, belongs to the Academy of Arts, Architecture and Design in Prague (Vysoká škola uměleckoprůmyslová v Praze).

THE FACULTY OF ARTS, CHARLES UNIVERSITY

Facing the bridge is the Neo-Classical building of the Faculty of Arts of Charles University, erected from 1924 to 1930 on a design by Josef Sakař. The land it is built on was part of Josefov (Josefstadt), the former Jewish town, before the slum clearance of the late nineteenth and the early twentieth century. The old houses were demolished together with the neighbouring blocks of Old Town, and, beginning in 1896, new buildings were erected in their place.

(149)

THE RUDOLFINUM

The most striking and most decorative façade on Palach Square is that of the Rudolfinum. This building is a fine example of the radical change in the perception of riverside land. In the mid-nineteenth century the riverbank still served as a place to dump rubbish; there was a prison here, a knacker's yard, warehouse yards, and a sawmill. But the plans for the Crown Prince Rudolph Embankment (today, the Aleš Embankment) led to a fundamental redevelopment of the area. In 1873 this piece of land was bought by the Česká spořitelna (Czech Savings Bank) with the intention of erecting connected buildings for concerts and exhibitions. The architectural competition was won by Josef Zítek and Josef Schulz, and the building was constructed from 1875 to 1881. Because Crown Prince Rudolph was the patron of the project and because it was erected on the embankment bearing his name, this building is called the Rudolfinum. In 1919–20 the interior was remodelled to serve the needs of the parliament of the Czechoslovak Republic. At present its two connected buildings again serve their original purposes: they house the exhibition rooms of the Galerie Rudolfinum and the concert hall of the Czech Philharmonic. Schulz also designed the nearby Museum of Decorative Arts, a Neo-Renaissance building erected in 1897–9.

Since 2000 a monument to the world-renowned composer Antonín Dvořák has stood in the little park across from the front entrance to the concert hall. It is the work of Josef Wagner (1901–1957) and his son Jan (1941–2005). The main concert hall here is also named after Dvořák, as is a section of the Vltava embankment in the direction of Na Františku.

THE PANORAMA OF PRAGUE CASTLE

For anyone walking through Prague, the view from Mánes Bridge across Klárov affords a monumental panorama of Prague Castle, together with the south-east side of the cathedral, that is, its oldest part, built by the master mason Matthew of Arras and his successor Peter Parler, and, below, a cluster of grand houses of the nobility. The two white steeples of the Basilica of St George rise up to the right of the cathedral.

The full name of the cathedral is the Church of St Vitus, St Wenceslas, and St Adalbert. It was founded by Charles IV and his father John of Luxembourg in 1344 as an expression of their reign, and was meant to serve as a place of coronations, pilgrimages, and memory, that is, as the burial place of the rulers of Bohemia. This cathedral, with its nave and two aisles, was not the first sanctuary at Prague Castle: it stands on the site of the former rotunda of St Vitus, which was founded in 930 by Duke Wenceslas, who became a patron saint of the Bohemian Lands. His successors then rebuilt it as a larger basilica.

The earliest part of the royal palace, built by the Přemyslids and the Luxembourgs, is located near the cathedral choir. The future rulers from the house of Jagiellon and, later, Habsburg added new buildings onto the Old Royal Palace towards the west. East of the cathedral is the large Rosenberg House, which, from 1755 to 1919, was the Theresian Foundation for Noblewomen (a Damenstift, where as many as thirty unmarried daughters of noble families could live as if in a religious order), and next to it is Lobkowicz House. The whole block terminates with the Black Tower, which guards one of the entrances to the Castle precinct. Around the Castle winds a ring of gardens, the most attractive of which are on the south side.

34A–C/ THE DVOŘÁK EMBANKMENT
(DVOŘÁKOVO NÁBŘEŽÍ)

The Dvořák Embankment was intended to follow on
smoothly from the construction of the Crown Prince Rudolph
Embankment, but was held up by a dispute with the Lanna
building company. The construction of this section of the
embankment did not therefore resume until 1899 and was not
finished until 1908. The quarter of a century which separates
the earlier from the later section of the embankment is, similarly
to the upper New Town riverside, revealed in their different
appearances: the later part reflects the new requirements
connected with barge traffic and making the river navigable.
Consequently, in the area called Na Františku, on the east section
of the Dvořák Embankment, ramps have been built providing
easy vehicle access to the quay, transit sheds, and moorings.

On the embankment between Čech Bridge and Štefánik
Bridge is the Hotel Intercontinental. It was built from 1968 to
1974 in the Brutalist style, on plans by Karel Filsak. He is also
the architect of the subsequent remodelling of an older building,
now the Hotel President, from 1969 to 1989.

The Neo-Classical building further downstream is the Na
Františku Hospital. It was erected from 1923 to 1927 on plans
by Vilém Kvasnička.

THE FACULTY OF LAW, CHARLES UNIVERSITY

The plot of land at the west end of Čech Bridge, which
became available for development after the slum clearance
of the late nineteenth and the early twentieth century, was
intended for the building of the Czech Faculty of Law at
Charles University. Its counterpart, east of the bridge, was
supposed to be the German Faculty of Law. The project
was assigned to the architect Jan Kotěra, but because his
plans were not accepted by everyone, and also because of
the First World War, construction work was delayed. In
the meantime, Kotěra abandoned his originally Late Art
Nouveau design, and tended instead to a Cubist and, then,
ultimately a Neo-Classical style. Kotěra died in 1923. When
construction work finally began in 1924, it was supervised by
his pupil, the architect Ladislav Machoň, and was finished
in 1931. After the Second World War and the expulsion of
the Czechoslovak Germans, the German Faculty of Law was
never built.

35A–C/ ČECH BRIDGE (ČECHŮV MOST)

The bridge, which in the extension of Pařížská třída (Paris Avenue) links Old Town with the road under the Letná hill, was built from 1906 to 1908 on plans by the architect Jan Koula. At that time the bold idea of extending the route from the bridge through a cutting in the Letná hill was being worked out. The iron bridge, which is named after the writer Svatopluk Čech, is in the Art Nouveau style with much sculptural ornamentation. On top of the pair of columns on each end of the bridge stand Antonín Popp's bronze allegorical figures of Victory. Other impressive bronze figures are located on the bridge piers nearer the water. On the west side, two female torch-bearers look down at the boats; on the east side, a pair of six-headed hydras, by the sculptors Ludvík Wurzel and Karel Opatrný, keep watch. The bridge has many other decorative features as well.

THE CHAPEL OF ST MARY MAGDALENE (KAPLE SV. MÁŘÍ MAGDALENY)

At the Letná Park end of Čech Bridge stands the small oval chapel of St Mary Magdalene. A work of Late Renaissance architecture, it was built in 1635. What is particularly interesting about the chapel is that it no longer stands on its original location: in the mid-1950s, as part of the alterations to the area at the end of the bridge and the Letná hill, together with the widening of the road below Letná, it was moved thirty metres upstream.

The most recent section of the Dvořák Embankment with the wide lower level and the moorings was not finished until 1908. The strip of riverbank is named after the Church of St Francis, part of the nearby Agnes Convent. Na Františku was originally surrounded by yards to which timber was brought by rafts and then worked on. Here, above the Helm Weir, was the traditional terminus for rafts and barges sailing from the upper course, because the river, with the weirs of the Petrská and Karlín districts, was difficult to navigate. The name of the district is derived from the Franciscan convent, a historic landmark of the embankment.

THE AGNES CONVENT (ANEŽSKÝ KLÁŠTER)

The convent, founded by Agnes of Bohemia (Anežka Přemyslovna) and Wenceslas I for the Poor Clares and Friars Minor, probably in 1231, is the first important Gothic building in Old Town. Among the oldest buildings of the convent, whose first Mother Superior was the Přemyslid princess Agnes of Bohemia, are the Church of St Francis and the convent of the Poor Clares. The second church, St Saviour, was intended as the burial place of the Přemyslids, which is why the mortal remains of some Přemyslid princesses and queens are buried in the crypt. Since taking care of the poor and the sick is among the services of the Poor Clares, the convent also had a hospital. Soon after its foundation, the convent became a centre of spiritual and cultural life in Bohemia. Despite its varied and complicated history, the convent has retained its Gothic appearance. After archaeological, architectural, and historical research in the first half of the twentieth century, the buildings were reconstructed and adapted for the National Gallery.

In the background of the photograph is historic architecture of Old Town, dominated by the double steeple of the Gothic Týn Church.

37A–B/ ŠTEFÁNIK BRIDGE (ŠTEFÁNIKŮV MOST)

The Štefánik Bridge, linking the boundary of Old Town and New Town on the right bank of the Vltava with the embankment below the Letná hill, replaced the Neo-Gothic chain bridge named after the Emperor Francis Joseph I, which had been built from 1865 to 1868. Since that bridge had ceased to meet the needs of transport, a temporary wooden bridge was built to the east of it in the course of the Second World War. From 1949 to 1951, the wooden bridge was replaced by one of reinforced concrete, designed by Vlastislav Hofman, who had also designed the Jirásek Bridge. Typical of both of his bridges is their elegant lightness.

At the Old Town end of Štefánik Bridge is the monumental building of the Ministry of Industry and Trade. It was built from 1928 to 1932 in a style combining elements of Late Art Nouveau and Neo-Classicism, on plans by Josef Fanta and with rich figural ornamentation by the sculptors Čeněk Vosmík and Josef A. Paukert. Contemporaries mocked the building because of its old-fashioned style, which was in strong contrast to the Functionalist buildings that were then in vogue.

The other end of the bridge, below the Letná hill, is perpendicular to the Edvard Beneš Embankment. The embankment wall, of Cyclopean masonry, was built after 1895 together with the new motorway. On the axis of the bridge, on the left bank, begins the arched portal of the Letná motorway tunnel. Opened to traffic in 1953, it has meant a substantial shortcut for motorists on their way from the centre of town to the north-west districts of Prague.

38/ THE NEW MILLS WATER TOWER
(NOVOMLÝNSKÁ VODÁRENSKÁ VĚŽ)

The east end of Štefánik Bridge, on the right bank in New Town, is dominated by the New Mills Water Tower, named after the Nové mlýny (New Mills), which once stood at the base of the tower. The riverbank here, as in the upper New Town, was completely covered with buildings used by a wide variety of trades, including three groups of mills. The tower had a wooden and a stone predecessor, neither of which withstood the onslaught of the Vltava floods. The current tower, dating from 1658, is built on the foundations of the previous tower, and, until 1877, supplied water to the lower New Town.

Of the mill buildings, only the Vávra Mill, no. 1239/2, has been preserved. Today, it is the Postal Museum. It was a Baroque building on Renaissance foundations, and its valuable current Neo-Classical appearance dates from about 1847. The interiors are decorated with paintings by Josef Navrátil. The area around the Vávra Mill and the little church of St Clement (sv. Klimenta, which has a Romanesque core) are a mixture of old, newish, and contemporary buildings.

39A,B/ THE ST PETER EMBANKMENT
(PETRSKÉ NÁBŘEŽÍ)

The St Peter Embankment is today called the nábřeží Ludvíka Svobody, that is, the Ludvík Svoboda Embankment, after a Czech general who was President of Czechoslovakia from 1968 to 1975. Running between Štefánik Bridge and Hlávka Bridge, it was built from 1908 to 1919 (work slowed down of course during the First World War), and it transformed this part of the city beyond recognition. All the small buildings used by the various trades were demolished to prepare for the planned radical land consolidation, which buttressed the bank and shifted it into the riverbed towards Primátorský ostrov (Mayor's Island) and Korunní ostrov (Crown Island). These long islands lining the riverbank were partly dug away on the side of the main river course, and the excavated earth was used to fill in the river arms and lagoons on the other side, thereby linking them to the mainland. Although they thus ceased to be islands, some of their surface continues to form part of the park in Lannova ulice (Lanna Street).

After declaring independence from Austria-Hungary in October 1918, the Czechoslovak Republic needed plots on which to erect buildings for its ministries and other State offices. The newly graded plots of land on the embankment were superbly suited to that purpose. The winners of the competition, held in 1919, for the architectural and urban-planning design of the New Town embankment between Štefánik Bridge and Hlávka Bridge were the

architects Antonín Engel and Bohumil Hübschmann.
Their design was for a set of government buildings in
the Neo-Classicist style, which both architects liked best.
In 1924–26 the Ministry of Public Works (later also a
health insurance company and a polyclinic designed by
Hübschmann) was built in Lannova ulice. It was, however,
only half the size of the vast building that was originally
planned, as is clear from the asymmetrical design of building
no. 1235/2. But two other blocks of these massive government
buildings close to Hlávka Bridge were finished: the Ministry
of Railways (today the Ministry of Transport and the Head
Office of Czech Rail) was built from 1922 to 1931 on plans
by Engel, and the Ministry of Agriculture, whose façade faces
Těšnov, was built from 1925 to 1932 on plans by František
Roith. The embankment here became calmer after motor
vehicle traffic was diverted into an underground tunnel in the
1980s.

THE POWER STATION ON ŠTVANICE

The western tip of the island called Štvanice was landscaped
in connection with the construction of the new Helm Weir
and lock from 1907 to 1912. An electric power station was
built on the island, from 1912 to 1915, in a style combining
elements of late Art Nouveau and Neo-Classicalism. A highly
harmonic focal point, its small scale makes the panoramas of
the office buildings on both riverbanks more subtle.

40A–D/ HLÁVKA BRIDGE (HLÁVKŮV MOST)

The need for a bridge to link New Town with Holešovice arose when the municipal slaughter house, today's Holešovice Market, was built on the riverbank at Holešovice in 1893–5. Until that time the only link was provided by footbridges between the individual little islands south of Štvanice, after which one had to take a ferry to the left bank. In 1900 the ferry was substituted for by a temporary wooden bridge. The southern part of the bridge link from Štvanice to New Town was not built until 1908–10. The section from Štvanice southwards was iron; for the northern part, from Štvanice to Holešovice, concrete could finally be used successfully. Consequently, the bridge named after the architect, entrepreneur, and philanthropist Josef Hlávka, which was opened in 1912, comprises two parts, each of different materials. The concrete half was designed in a geometrically modern style by the architect Pavel Janák. Above the water level, the bridge piers are decorated with relief sculptures of male and female figures by Bohumil Kafka and Ladislav Kofránek. The faces of the arches over the river are decorated with medallions of important men who participated in the building of the bridge; they are the work of the sculptors Josef Mařatka and Otto Gutfreund. The Holešovice end of the bridge has two sculptural groups by Jan Štursa on the themes of Labour and Humanity. From 1958 to 1962, the whole bridge was totally remodelled on plans by the architect Stanislav Hubička. At that time, the iron part of the bridge was also replaced with a concrete structure.

From Hlávka Bridge, one can descend to Štvanice, whose name reminds us that blood sports, such as baiting animals and forcing them to fight each other, were held here in a wooden arena, particularly in the seventeenth century, as entertainment for the upper classes. In the nineteenth century, Štvanice, particularly because of the dances organized here in open-air restaurants, was long a popular destination for excursions. Since the twentieth century, the island has been used mainly for sports.

41A–D/ LETNÁ PARK (LETENSKÉ SADY)

Letná Park was made on the slopes north of what is today the
Edvard Beneš Embankment and on part of the Letná plain
from 1860 to 1864. It is accessible from the embankment
by the steps opposite Čech Bridge. An essential part of the
design was the paths with lookout points affording fine views
of the city and the river with its bridges. In connection with
the Bohemian Centenary Exposition of Industry in 1891, the
area was comprehensively landscaped under the direction of
the landscape architect František Thomayer. What remains
of his design today is chiefly the grand lane bordered with
plane trees.

THE HANAU PAVILION
(HANAVSKÝ PAVILON)

This charming little building in a mainly Neo-Baroque style is made of cast iron, concrete, and glass. It was originally built in 1891 to represent the Komárov Ironworks (south-west of Prague), owned by Wilhelm von Hanau-Hořovice, at the Bohemian Centenary Exhibition of Industry, held on the Exhibition Grounds (Výstaviště) in Prague. After the exhibition, the owner of the pavilion presented it to the City of Prague, and it has since become a Letná landmark.

THE PRAGUE METRONOME

In the 1950s, on the highest of the lookout points on the western end of the extended axis of Čech Bridge stood a gigantic monument to Joseph Stalin. The monument was demolished in 1962, nine years after Stalin's death, but its huge pedestal, including underground chambers, and the double flight of steps leading up to it from the embankment, have remained. The monument, comprising eight figures standing double file behind Generalissimo Stalin, was popularly derided as the 'queue for meat'(a foodstuff in short supply at the time). After the crimes of the Stalinist period were revealed in Moscow in 1956, the monument was finally removed. On the pedestal, which also serves as a lookout point, a giant metronome by the sculptor Vratislav Novák was installed in 1991.

42/ THE VIEW OF PRAGUE BRIDGES FROM LETNÁ PARK

When looking south from the Letná hill, one can see
Mánes Bridge, Charles Bridge, the Bridge of the Legions,
Jirásek Bridge, and, in the distance, Palacký Bridge. Nine
of the many bridges over the Vltava at Prague were made
in the course of only 53 years, from 1878 to 1931. Their
design was entrusted to architects, some of whom were

leading proponents of the Avant-garde. All these bridges, without exception, today constitute an extraordinary set of architecture, which deserves not only our attention but also, indeed mainly, suitable preservation.

The bridges over the Vltava at Prague have often been compared to the strings of a harp – in their individual details they may differ, but the rhythm of their arches creates a visual harmony.

(175)

THE ISLANDS, BRIDGES, AND EMBANKMENTS OF THE VLTAVA AT PRAGUE

THE ISLANDS (from south to north)

1. Veslařský ostrov (Rowers' Island, Podolí)   The earliest record of the island dates from the fifteenth century. The Schwarzenbergs built a port here for rafts sailing from their estates in south Bohemia, and that's why the island used to be called Švarcenberský ostrov. It was renamed in 1952, reflecting its new use as a base from which to do water sports.

2. Císařská louka (Emperor's Mead, Smíchov)   This island was made, from 1899 to 1903, when part of the large floodplain was separated from the mainland by creating a river arm for a raft port. It is still used for sport and other recreation.

3. Petržilkovský ostrov (Petržilka Island, Smíchov)   The first record of this little island, on which mills and, since 1502, the Lesser Town Water Tower have stood, dates from the fourteenth century. It was named after a late-fifteenth-century mill owner. The surface area of the island was reduced when the lock was built from 1911 to 1922.

4. Dětský ostrov (Children's Island, Smíchov)   This island first appears in the records in the mid-fourteenth century. It was originally called Maltézský ostrov (Maltese Island), because it belonged to the Knights of Malta. In the nineteenth century it began to be called Židovský ostrov (Jews Island) because it belonged to a Jewish family. Today's name refers to the children's playgrounds built here after 1960.

5. Slovanský ostrov (Slav Island, in New Town)   This island was created by alluvial deposits in the seventeenth and eighteenth centuries. Its original name, Barvířský ostrov (or, popularly, Barvířka**)** was derived from the dyeworks that were in operation here. It was also called Šítkovský ostrov, after Šítka, the owner of the local mills, and also Engelův ostrov, after Engel, the owner of a factory for chintz (printed calico) or fancy cotton and an inn. The name Žofín ostrov was officially given to the island in 1838 in honour of the Archduchess Sophie of Austria (Žofie, in Czech). The island was renamed Slovanský ostrov in 1925 to commemorate the Pan-Slav Congress of 1848, which was held in the hall of the local inn.

6. Střelecký ostrov (Sharpshooter Island, in Old Town)   The first record of this island dates from the fourteenth century. In the course of its history it has had a number of names, including Malé Benátky (Little Venice, unlike the Štvanice Island, which was called Velké Benátky), Hořejší ostrov (Upper Island, as opposed to Dolejší ostrov,

Lower Island, as Kampa used to be called), Trávník (Lawn), and Vodní dvůr (Water-side Hall). Because this is where the Prague Sharpshooters Corps traditionally had its shooting range, the name Střelecký ostrov has stuck since the nineteenth century.

7. Kampa (in Lesser Town) This island was made when part of the Lesser Town riverbank was separated from the mainland by digging a river arm. This arm was given the name Čertovka (the Devil's Mill Race), and already in the twelfth century it was already in operation to drive a mill wheel. In the course of the centuries, Kampa was called the Ostrov (Island) or Dolní ostrov (Lower Island). It was not generally called Kampa until the eighteenth century; the origin of the name is unclear, but may well come from the Latin *campus* or the Old Czech word *zákampí* (a shady place), or even a man who owned a house here in the seventeenth century.

8. Křižovnický ostrov (Knights of the Cross Island, in Old Town) This small inaccessible island is situated between Charles Bridge and the monastery of the Knights of the Cross. By 1170 at the latest, the Tower of the Romanesque Judith Bridge stood here. The tower later became part of the monastery building on the Old Town riverbank.

9. Štvanice (Blood-sport Island, in Holešovice) This is the largest of the Prague islands, and has been in existence from at least the earliest years of the town. Its current name is derived from an arena in which blood sports (*štvanice zvířat*) were held for the amusement of the nobility from the seventeenth to the beginning of the nineteenth century. It was also known as the Veliký ostrov (Greater Island) and Velké Benátky (Greater Venice). It was called Venice because to the south there were five other, smaller islands, which ceased to exist when the Petrské nábřeží (today, St Peter's Embankment and the nábřeží Ludvíka Svobody, that is, Ludvík Svoboda Embankment) was built and the river was made navigable.

10. Primátorský ostrov (Mayor's Island, in New Town) This island, which no longer exists, once lined the riverbank of the New Town and, between the New Mills and the Lodecký Mills, formed an almost fully enclosed lagoon. It was called Primátorský because it referred to a time when it belonged to the office of the mayor (*primátor*) of New Town. Part of the island has vanished, and another part is incorporated into the New Town riverside, now the Ludvík Svoboda Embankment.

11. Korunní ostrov (Crown Island, in New Town and Karlín) This island no longer exists either. It used to be linked to Primátorský ostrov, and bordered the riverbank south of Štvanice Island. It was used for agriculture, for example, the cultivation of horseradish, and its Czech name was the result of a bad translation or corruption of its German name, Kreninsel (that is, Horseradish Island). Part of the island vanished; another part was incorporated into the New Town riverbank.

12. Jerusalémský ostrov (Jerusalem Island, in Karlín) Like the other islands south of Štvanice, this now defunct island was made by alluvial deposits, and, like those islands, its riverbanks, owners, and names also changed. At the end of the eighteenth century, Johann Ferdinand von Schönfeld established pleasure gardens here, with an inn, a dance hall, and a theatre, which was called Růžodol (Rosenthal, in German), and hence the island was called Růžodolský. In the nineteenth century, the buildings were changed into a bleachery for calico, owned by Moses Jerusalem. Beginning in 1870, the island was connected to the neighbouring Rohanský ostrov because of the railway, and thus became part of it.

13. Rohanský ostrov (Rohan Island, in Karlín) Another now no-longer-extant island, Rohanský ostrov was named after its owner in the mid-nineteenth century, the carpenter Jan Rohan. (Previously, it had been called Köpplovský ostrov). After Jerusalem Island and Rohan Island were joined, they were called Rohanský ostrov. Beginning in 1870, this island was used by the Austrian North-West Rail Company to lead a section of track from Těšnov to Karlín and to establish a goods station. After an arm of the river at the Karlín port was filled in 1954, Rohanský ostrov became part of the Karlín riverbank.

14. Kamenský ostrov (in Karlín) No longer extant, this small island had a mill called Na Kameni, which in the sixteenth century was owned by the miller Martin Šašek. Whereas the first name of the island comes from the name of the mill, the second name, Šaškovský, comes from the name of the miller. Ever since the arm of the river was filled in, the island has been part of the mainland.

15. Buriánka (in Karlín) This small island, no longer extant, was easily accessible by footbridges from the mainland. In the sixteenth century the Old Town paper mill was located here, and so the island was called Papírnický ostrov. In the seventeenth century the paper mill was replaced by František's Buriánek's flour mill, with a garden open to the public, and the island was then named after the owner. Later, other industries were established here. When the arm of the river was filled in, this island too became part of the mainland.

16. Libeňský ostrov (in Libeň) This is the largest of the islands that were formed by the river in the Holešovice meander and were also changed by frequent floods. After the regulation of the riverbed in 1930, the island was joined to the territory of the Prague districts of Libeň and Karlín, and thus became a peninsula.

17. Holešovický ostrov (in Troja) This large island no longer exists. Actually a part of the riverside floodplain at Troja, it was separated from the mainland by an arm of the Vltava. Fruit and vegetables used to be grown here. Today, incorporated into the mainland, the area is interwoven with a number of transportation routes, including the Vltava motorway, one end of the Troja Bridge, and one end of the Blanka Tunnel.

18. Císařský ostrov (Emperor's Island, in Dejvice and Bubeneč) The Bohemian estates gave this island to the Emperor Rudolph II, who had a gem-cutting workshop, a mill, and a summer house built here. The island in those days, however, was bigger and had a different shape from today's. In about 1900, a canal was dug through the island and part of the surface of the original island around Císařský mlýn (Emperor's Mill) was incorporated into the mainland. In the western part of the island is a Prague water treatment plant.

19. Trojský ostrov (in Troja) No longer an island. Part of the bank of the Vltava at Troja was originally separated from the mainland by an arm of the river. As early as in the sixteenth century, a mill was established there, which in the mid-nineteenth century was remodelled as a granary. The mill race, which had become redundant, was filled in when the river was regulated in the late nineteenth and the early twentieth century. The former island is now the home of Prague Zoo.

THE BRIDGES (in chronological order)

1. Judith Bridge, completed *c.*1172, was destroyed by a flood in 1342. Made of stone, with arches. Was roughly where the Charles Bridge stands today.

2. Charles Bridge (Karlův most), the foundation stone was laid in 1357; work was completed *c.*1380. Made of stone, with arches. The master mason was probably Peter Parler. Originally called Stone Bridge or Prague Bridge, it has been called Charles Bridge only since 1870.

3. Francis I Bridge, built from 1839 to 1841; dismantled in 1898. An iron suspension bridge, it was designed by Bedřich Schnirch. Today, the Bridge of the Legions stands in its place (see no. 11, below).

4. Railway Viaduct, built from 1846 to 1850. Made of stone and with arches, it was designed by Alois Negrelli.

5. Francis Joseph I Bridge, built from 1865 to 1868; demolished in 1947. This iron suspension bridge was designed by Rowland Mason Ordish and William Henry Le Feuvre; its architect was Max am Ende. In 1891, at the time of the Bohemian Centenary Exhibition of Industry, the bridge was reinforced with a temporary wooden structure, which was also used for the overhaul of the bridge, and was then taken down in 1900. It was called Štefánik Bridge (1919–40), Leoš Janáček Bridge during the German occupation (1940–45); and was again called Štefánik Bridge (1945–47). Today, a new Štefánik Bridge stands in its place (see no. 21, below).

6. Crown Prince Rudolph Footbridge, built in 1868–69, taken down in 1914. This iron suspension bridge was designed by Karl Ritter von Wessely (Karel rytíř Veselý), using the Ordish-Lefeuvre system. It was also known variously as the Rudolph Bridge, the Iron Bridge, and the Chain Bridge. Today, the Mánes Bridge stands roughly in its place (see no. 16, below).

7. The Railway Bridge below Vyšehrad. The original bridge was built in 1871, and demolished in 1901. An iron truss bridge, it was designed by the Harkort Company of Duisburg. (For the railway bridge that replaced, see no. 12, below).

8. Palacký Bridge (Palackého most), built in 1876–78. A stone arch bridge, it was designed by Josef Reiter; the architecture is by Bedřich Münzberger; and the decoration is by Josef Václav Myslbek. The four sculptural groups decorating both ends of the bridge were put in place from 1889 to 1897; immediately after the Second World War, they were moved to Vyšehrad. From 1940 to 1945, during the German occupation, it was called Mozart Bridge. Since then, it has been called by its original name.

9. The Temporary Francis I Bridge, built in 1898, dismantled in 1901. This wooden truss bridge was designed by Jiří Soukup. It was used for the dismantling of the Francis I Chain Bridge (see no. 3, above) and the construction of the new stone bridge of the same name (see no. 11, below).

10. The Temporary Bridge across Štvanice, built in 1901; dismantled in 1912. A wooden truss bridge, designed by Rudolf Kaplan. It was used before Hlávka Bridge was built and also during the construction of that bridge (see no. 15, below).

11. Bridge of the Legions, built from 1898 to 1901 to take the place of the suspension bridge of the same name (see no. 3, above). This stone arch bridge was designed by Jiří Soukup; its architecture is by Antonín Balšánek. Originally called the Francis I Bridge, it was later called the Bridge of the Legions (Most Legií, 1919–40), and, during the German occupation, Smetana Bridge (1940–45), and then the Bridge of the Legions (1945–60), but for the next thirty years May Day Bridge (Prvního máje, 1960–90). It is now again the Bridge of the Legions (since 1990).

12. The Railway Bridge below Vyšehrad (Železniční most pod Vyšehradem), built in 1901, replaced the earlier railway bridge (see no. 7, above). This iron truss bridge was designed and built by Prášil Brothers bridge-building company in Libeň.

13. The Temporary Libeň Bridge, built in 1903, taken down in 1928. A mostly wooden truss arch bridge, made with additional reinforced concrete. Was built partly from the dismantled structure of the temporary bridge that led from the National Theatre to Smíchov (see no. 9, above), and partly by extending it since the river is wider here. It was designed by Jiří Soukup. The reinforced-concrete arch in the Libeň part was designed by Václav Trča. Today, the Libeň Bridge stands in its place (see no. 17, below).

14. Svatopluk Čech Bridge (Most Svatopluka Čecha, today called Čechův most), built from 1905 to 1908. This iron, arch bridge was designed by the engineers Zdeněk Bažant and Jan Kolář of the Bridge-building Department of Prague City Hall and the architect Jan Koula, with ornamentation by Antonín Popp, Ludvík Herzl, Karel Opatrný, and Ludvík Wurzel. Between 1940 and 1945, during the German occupation, it was called Gregor Mendel Bridge. Since 1945 it has been called Čech Bridge.

15. Hlávka Bridge (Hlávkův most). The part leading from a point on the boundary between New Town and Karlín to Štvanice Island was built from 1908 to 1910 as an iron arched bridge on a design by Jiří Soukup. This part was dismantled in 1960 and replaced by a wider, reinforced-concrete bridge. The part of the bridge between Štvanice and Holešovice was built from 1910 to 1912 as a concrete arch bridge. It was designed by the engineer František Mencl and the architect Pavel Janák, with ornamentation by Jan Štursa, Josef Mařatka, and Otto Gutfreund. The bridge was widened in 1958–62.

16. Mánes Bridge (Mánesův most). This concrete arch bridge was built from 1911 to 1914 to take the place of the Chain Footbridge (see no. 6, above). It was designed by the engineer František Mencl and the architect Mečislav Petrů, with ornamentation by František Bílek, Josef Mařatka, and Jan Štursa.

17. Libeň Bridge (Libeňský most), built 1924–28. This concrete arch bridge was designed by the engineer František Mencl and the architect Pavel Janák. It was called Baxa Bridge (1938–40), and, during the German occupation, Libeň Bridge (1940–45), and then again Baxa Bridge (1945–52), but for ten years it was called Stalingrad Bridge (1952–62). Today it is once again called Libeň Bridge (since 1962).

18. Troja Bridge, built in 1926–28. This reinforced-concrete arch bridge with a composite bridge deck was dismantled in 1977. It was designed by the engineer František Mencl and the architect Josef Chochol. From 1946 until it was dismantled, it was called Barricade-fighters Bridge (Most Barikádníků). In its place stands the new Barricade-fighters Bridge (see no. 26, below).

19. Jirásek Bridge (Jiráskův most), built in 1929–33. This reinforced-concrete arch bridge with a composite bridge deck was designed by the engineer František Mencl and the architect Vlastislav Hofman. during the German occupation it was called Dientzenhofer Bridge (1940–45). Since the end of war it is Jirásek Bridge.

20. The Temporary Janáček Bridge, built in 1941, dismantled in 1953. This wooden girder bridge was designed by the engineer František Mencl. It was used after the iron Janáček Bridge (originally the Francis Joseph I Bridge, see no. 5, above) was no longer used for vehicles and before Šverma Bridge was built (see no. 21, below).

21. Šverma Bridge, today the **Štefánik Bridge** (Štefánikův most), built in 1949–53. This reinforced-concrete arch bridge with a composite bridge deck was designed by the engineer Oldřich Širc and the architect Vlastislav Hofman. Built to take the place of the iron Štefánik Bridge (originally the Francis Joseph I Bridge, see no. 5, above). In 1997, it was renamed Štefánik Bridge.

22. Braník Railway Bridge (Branický železniční most), built from 1949 to 1955. This reinforced-concrete arch bridge was designed by the engineers Jiří Klimeš, Zbyšek Krušina, and Vladislav Valoušek. Because it was built partly by a number of people who under the Communist régime were forced to make their living as manual labourers, it was popularly called the Bridge of the Intelligentsia (Most inteligence).

23. The Temporary Barricade-fighters Bridge, built in 1970, dismantled in 1980. This steel truss bridge was replaced by the new Barricade-fighters Bridge (see no. 26, below) in 1980.

24. The Temporary Tramway Bridge between Holešovice and Troja, built in 1977, dismantled in 2014. A steel girder bridge, it was replaced in 1981 by a truss bridge. Popularly known as Rámusák (that is, Pandemonium).

25. The Railway Bridge below Bulovka (Železniční most pod Bulovkou), built in 1973–76. This bridge of pre-stressed concrete was designed by the Stavby silnic a železnic (Road and Railway Construction) company.

26. Barricade-fighters Bridge (Most Barikádníků), built 1977–80. This steel girder bridge was designed by Jiří Trnka and Petr Dobrovský.

27. Antonín Zápotocký Bridge (Most Antonína Zápotockého, today the **Barrandov Bridge** (Barrandovský most), built from 1978 to 1988. This pre-stressed concrete and girder bridge was designed by the engineers Jiří Hejnic and Pavel Tripl and the architect Karel Filsak. Its decoration is by Josef Klimeš. In 1990, it was renamed Barrandov Bridge.

28. Troja Footbridge (Trojská lávka), built in 1984. This concrete suspension bridge was designed by Jiří Stráský. It took the place of the temporary pontoon bridge from the 1970s, which had been damaged in the flood of 1977.

29. Troja Bridge (Trojský most), built from 2009 to 2014. This concrete arch bridge with a lower bridge deck was designed by the engineering firm of Mott MacDonald (Jiří Petrák and Ladislav Špaček) and the architects Roman Koucký and Libor Kábrt.

Most of the facts here have been taken from Jan Fischer and Ondřej Fischer, *Pražské mosty*, Prague: Academia, 1985.

THE EMBANKMENTS (listed chronologically)

1. Smetana Embankment (Smetanovo nábřeží), built in 1841–45. Originally called simply the Nábřeží (Embankment), because there was no other embankment in Prague, or, alternatively, the Staroměstské nábřeží (Old Town Embankment). Its official names have been Františkovo nábřeží (the Francis Embankment, 1894–1919), the Masarykovo nábřeží (Masaryk Embankment, 1919–42), the Reinhard-Heydrich-Ufer (1942–45), the Masaryk Embankment (1945–52), and the Smetana Embankment (since 1952).

2. Janáček Embankment (Janáčkovo nábřeží), **north part**, built in 1874–75. Over the years its official names have been the Ferdinandovo nábřeží (Ferdinand Embankment, 1874–1919), the nábřeží Legií (Legions Embankment, 1919–40), the Pekařovo nábřeží (the Pekař Embankment, 1940–45), the nábřeží Legií (Legions Embankment, 1945–52), and the Janáčkovo nábřeží (Janáček Embankment, since 1952).

3. Aleš Embankment (Alšovo nábřeží), built in 1875–77. Over the years it has officially been called the Dolní nábřeží (Lower Embankment, 1870–78), the Nábřeží korunního prince Rudolfa (Crown Prince Rudolph Embankment, 1878–1919), and the Alšovo nábřeží (Aleš Embankment, since 1919).

4. Rašín Embankment (Rašínovo nábřeží), **north part**, built from 1876 to 1879. Over the years it has been called the Palackého nábřeží (Palacký Embankment, 1876–1940), the Vltavské nábřeží (Vltava Embankment, 1940–42), the Reinhard-Heydrich-Ufer (1942–45), then back to the Palacký Embankment (1945–51), the Nábřeží Bedřicha Engelse (Friedrich Engels Embankment, 1951–90), and the Rašín Embankment (since 1990).

5. The Lower Town Embankment (Malostranské nábřeží), built in 1905. This has been its official name from the beginning.

6. Edvard Beneš Embankment (Nábřeží Edvarda Beneše), built in 1895–6. Over the years it has officially been called the 'motorway below Letná Hill' (1896–1920), the 'embankment below Letná Hill' (1920–37), the Kramářovo nábřeží (Kramář Embankment, 1938–48), the nábřeží Kapitána Jaroše (Captain Jaroš Embankment, 1948–91), and the Nábřeží Edvarda Beneše (Edvard Beneš Embankment, since 1991) (the part between Klárov and Štefánikův most).

7. Dvořák Embankment (Dvořákovo nábřeží), built from 1899 to 1908. This has been its official name since 1904.

8. Masaryk Embankment (Masarykovo nábřeží), built in 1903–05. Over the years it has officially been called the Riegrovo nábřeží (Rieger Embankment, 1903–40), the

Vltavské nábřeží (Vltava Embankment, 1940–42), the Reinhard-Heydrich-Ufer (1942–45), briefly back to Riegrovo (1945–46), then the Gottwaldovo nábřeží (Gottwald Embankment, 1946–90), and the Masarykovo nábřeží (since 1990).

9. **Rašín Embankment** (Rašínovo nábřeží), **south part**, built in 1904–07. Over the years it has officially been called the Vyšehradské nábřeží (Vyšehrad Embankment, 1905–19), the Podskalské nábřeží (Podskalí Embankment, 1919–24), the Rašínovo nábřeží (Rašín Embankment, 1924–41) (connected with the Libuše Embankment by the tunnel in Podolí), the Nábřeží Karla Lažnovského (Karel Lažnovský, 1941–45), back to the Rašín Embankment (1945–51), the Nábřeží Bedřicha Engelse (Friedrich Engels Embankment, 1951–90) (separated from the Podolí Embankment and connected to the Palacký Embankment), and is the Rašín Embankment once again (since 1990).

10. **Podolí Embankment** (Podolské nábřeží), **north part**, built from 1904 to 1907. Over the years it has officially been called Vyšehradské nábřeží (Vyšehrad Embankment, 1904–06), the Libušino nábřeží (Libuše Embankment, 1906–24), the Rašínovo nábřeží (Rašín Embankment, 1924–41) (connected with Podskalské nábřeží north of the tunnel), the Nábřeží Karla Lažnovského (Karel Lažnovský Embankment, 1941–45), the Rašín Embankment again (1945–51), and the Karl Marx Embankment (1951–90). It has been part of the Podolí Embankment (Podolské nábřeží) since 1990.

11. **The Capitan Jaroš Embankment** (Nábřeží kapitána Jaroše), built in 1908–10. Over the years, this has had several official names: originally part of Bělského ulice (Bělský street) on the west side and Vltavská ulice (Vltava street) on the east side, it was part of the Kramář Embankment (Kramářovo nábřeží, 1938–48), and has carried its current name since 1948, given to the whole bank from below Letná to Klárov. Since 1991, however, only the part between Štefánik Bridge and Hlávka Bridge is still called Nábřeží Kapitána Jaroše.

12. **Bubny Embankment** (Bubenské nábřeží), built in 1908–10. From 1908 to 1930, it was called Vltavská ulice (Vltava Street). It has had its present name since 1930.

13. **Ludvík Svoboda Embankment** (Nábřeží Ludvíka Svobody), built in 1908–19. Over the years it has been officially called the Petrské nábřeží (St Peter's Embankment, 1919–34), the Švehlovo nábřeží (Švehla Embankment, 1934–48), the Nábřeží První čs. Kyjevské brigády (Embankment of the First Czechoslovak Kiev Brigade (1948–61), and the nábřeží Kyjevské brigády (Embankment of the Kiev Brigade, 1961–79). It has had its present name since 1979.

14. **The Upper Embankment** (Hořejší nábřeží), originally a riverside road, it was called Hořejší ulice from 1880 onwards. The embankment was built from 1925 to 1929.

15. **Podolí Embankment** (Podolské nábřeží), **south part**, built in 1935. It has always had this name.

Note: this list of Prague embankments on the Vltava does not include the Kosárek Embankment (Kosárkovo nábřeží), which is actually only a riverside road running by the Straka Academy rather than an embankment in the true sense of the word. The information about the changes of place names is drawn from Marek Laštovka et al., *Pražský uličník: Encyklopedie názvů pražských veřejných prostranství*, vols 1 and 2, Prague: Libri, 1997.

THE STATUES ON CHARLES BRIDGE, PRAGUE
(In the order from the left, on the Old Town side, to Lesser Town)

1. St Ivo. Matthias Bernhard Braun, 1711, sandstone, copy 1908. The original sculptural group is in the Lapidarium of the National Museum, Prague.

2. The Blessed Virgin Mary and St Bernard. Mathias Wenzel Jäckel, 1709, sandstone; copy 1978–80. The original sculptural group is in Gorlice Hall, Vyšehrad, Prague.

3. Sts Barbara, Margaret the Virgin, and Elizabeth of Hungary, Johann Brokoff and Ferdinand Maximilian Brokoff, 1707, sandstone.

4. The Blessed Virgin Mary, St Thomas Aquinas, and St Dominic, Mathias Wenzel Jäckel, 1708, sandstone; copy 1958–61. The original sculptural group is in the Lapidarium of the National Museum, Prague.

5. *Pietà*, Emanuel Max, 1859, sandstone. A column shrine stood here in the Middle Ages. In about 1700, a sculptural group of the *Pietà* by Johann Brokoff was installed, but was damaged during the June 1848 uprising. Today, the original Brokoff sculpture is on the courtyard of the Sisters of Mercy of St Borromeo Hospital (Pod Petřínem), Prague.

6. The Crucifixion (Calvary). Wolf Ernst Brohn (body of Christ), 1629, bronze; George Heermann (the little hill with inscribed plaques), 1707, sandstone; Emanuel Max, 1861, sandstone (the two statues on the sides). Already when the bridge was made, a cross was placed here, but because it was in such poor shape it was replaced. In 1629, figures of saints were added to the Cross, allegedly painted on wooden panels. The current sculpture of the body of Christ was cast in Dresden in 1629, and placed on the bridge in 1657. The figures of the Mater Dolorosa and St John the Evangelist below the cross were exchanged in 1866 for lead statues and again in 1861 for the current ones by Emanuel Max. The abusive inscription in Hebrew, placed on the cross in 1696, was paid for with money from a fine that a certain Jew had to pay for having allegedly mocked the cross.

7. St Joseph with the Christ Child. Emanuel Max, 1854, sandstone. The original statue of St Joseph with the Christ Child was probably made by Michael Johann Joseph Brokoff in 1706. After being damaged in the uprising of 1848, it was removed, and its fate remains unknown.

8. St Anne. Mathias Wenzel Jäckel, 1707, sandstone; copy 1999. The original sculptural group is in Gorlice Hall, Vyšehrad, Prague.

9. St Francis Xavier. Ferdinand Maximilian Brokoff, 1711, sandstone; copy 1913. The sculptural group came crashing down into the Vltava when the flood swept away parts of Charles Bridge in 1890. A copy was made from the damaged work, in 1913, by the sculptor Čeněk Vosmík. The torso of the original sculptural group is in the Lapidarium of the National Museum, Prague.

10. Sts Cyril and Methodius. Karel Dvořák, 1928–38, sandstone. A sculptural group of St Ignatius of Loyola by Ferdinand Maximilian Brokoff, from 1709, originally stood on this place, but it collapsed into the Vltava when the flood of September 1890 swept away parts of Charles Bridge. The remains of the original sculptural group are in the Lapidarium of the National Museum, Prague.

11. St Christopher. Emanuel Max, 1857, sandstone. Originally, a sentry post stood on this place, but it collapsed into the Vltava in the flood of 1784.

12. St John the Baptist. Josef Max, 1855, sandstone. Originally a sculpture of the Baptism of Christ, from the workshop of Johann Brokoff, 1706, stood here, but it was damaged in 1848. The original sculptural group is in the Lapidarium of the National Museum, Prague.

13. St Francis Borgia. Ferdinand Maximilian Brokoff, 1710, sandstone. The statue is currently in the care of restorers.

14. Sts Norbert, Wenceslas, and Sigismund. Josef Max, 1853, sandstone. The present sculptural group was preceded by two versions of the group with St Norbert. The original, by F. M. Brokoff, from 1708, was damaged, probably during the Prussian siege in 1757, and was replaced in 1765 with a group by Ignaz Franz Platzer. The two earlier sculptural groups are now missing.

15. St Ludmila of Bohemia. Matthias Bernard Braun, 1720, sandstone, copy 1999. Originally, a statue of St Wenceslas by Ottavio Mosto stood on this place, but was swept into the Vltava during the flood of 1784. It was replaced by Braun's statue of St Ludmila, which was moved from its original place on the ramp at Prague Castle. The original sculptural group of St Wenceslas is now in the Lapidarium of the National Museum, Prague. Braun's original St Ludmila is exhibited in Gorlice Hall, Vyšehrad, Prague.

16. St John Nepomucene. Johann Brokoff, after 1681, bronze. The only bronze statue on the bridge.

17. St Francis of Assisi. Emanuel Max, 1855, sandstone. Originally a sculptural group by Franz Preiss from 1708 stood here. The individual sculptures are today in the Church of St Joseph, on náměstí Republiky, Prague.

18. St Anthony of Padua. Johann Ulrich Mayer, 1707, sandstone.

19. St Procopius of Sázava and St Vincent Ferrer. Ferdinand Maximilian Brokoff, 1712, sandstone. The sculptural group is in the care of restorers.

20. St Jude the Apostle. Johann Ulrich Mayer, 1708, sandstone.

21. St Nicholas of Tolentino. Hieronymus Kohl, 1708, sandstone, copy 1970. The original is today exhibited in Gorlice Hall, Vyšehrad, Prague.

22. St Augustine of Hippo. Hieronymus Kohl, 1708, sandstone, copy 1971. The original of the statue is today exhibited in Gorlice Hall, Vyšehrad, Prague.

23. St Lutgardis of Aywières. Matthias Bernard Braun, 1710, sandstone; copy 1995. The original sculptural group is in the Lapidarium of the National Museum, Prague.

24. St Cajetan. Ferdinand Maximilian Brokoff, 1709, sandstone.

25. St Adalbert. Ferdinand Maximilian Brokoff, 1709, sandstone, 1973. The original is today in Gorlice Hall, Vyšehrad, Prague.

26. St Philip Benitius. Bernhard Michael Mandl, marble, 1714.

27. St John of Matha, St Felix of Valois, and the Blessed Ivan. Ferdinand Maximilian Brokoff, sandstone, 1714.

28. St Vitus. Ferdinand Maximilian Brokoff, 1714, sandstone.

29. St Wenceslas. Josef Kamil Böhm, 1859, sandstone. Originally no statue stood here at the Lesser Town end of the bridge.

30. St Saviour, Sts Cosmas and Damian. Johann Ulrich Mayer, sandstone, 1709.

Source: Pavla Státníková, Ondřej Šefců, and Zdeněk Dragoun, *Kamenný most v Praze: Obrazové svědectví historie Juditina a Karlova mostu*, Prague: Muzeum hl. m. Prahy, 2013.

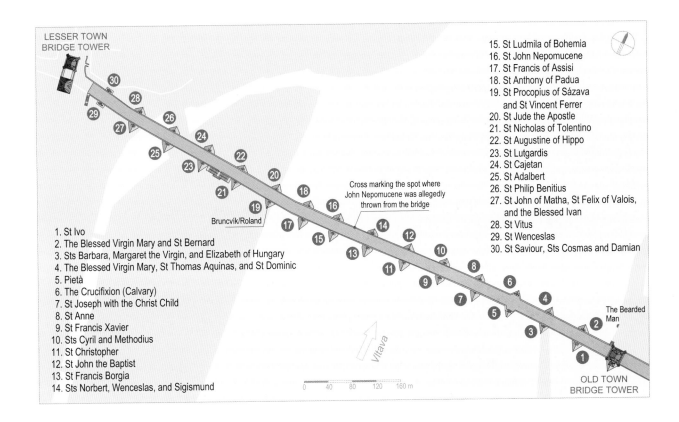

LESSER TOWN
BRIDGE TOWER

15. St Ludmila of Bohemia
16. St John Nepomucene
17. St Francis of Assisi
18. St Anthony of Padua
19. St Procopius of Sázava
    and St Vincent Ferrer
20. St Jude the Apostle
21. St Nicholas of Tolentino
22. St Augustine of Hippo
23. St Lutgardis
24. St Cajetan
25. St Adalbert
26. St Philip Benitius
27. St John of Matha, St Felix of Valois,
    and the Blessed Ivan
28. St Vitus
29. St Wenceslas
30. St Saviour, Sts Cosmas and Damian

Cross marking the spot where
John Nepomucene was allegedly
thrown from the bridge

Bruncvík/Roland

1. St Ivo
2. The Blessed Virgin Mary and St Bernard
3. Sts Barbara, Margaret the Virgin, and Elizabeth of Hungary
4. The Blessed Virgin Mary, St Thomas Aquinas, and St Dominic
5. Pietà
6. The Crucifixion (Calvary)
7. St Joseph with the Christ Child
8. St Anne
9. St Francis Xavier
10. Sts Cyril and Methodius
11. St Christopher
12. St John the Baptist
13. St Francis Borgia
14. Sts Norbert, Wenceslas, and Sigismund

The Bearded
Man

OLD TOWN
BRIDGE TOWER

Vltava

0   40   80   120   160 m

(187)

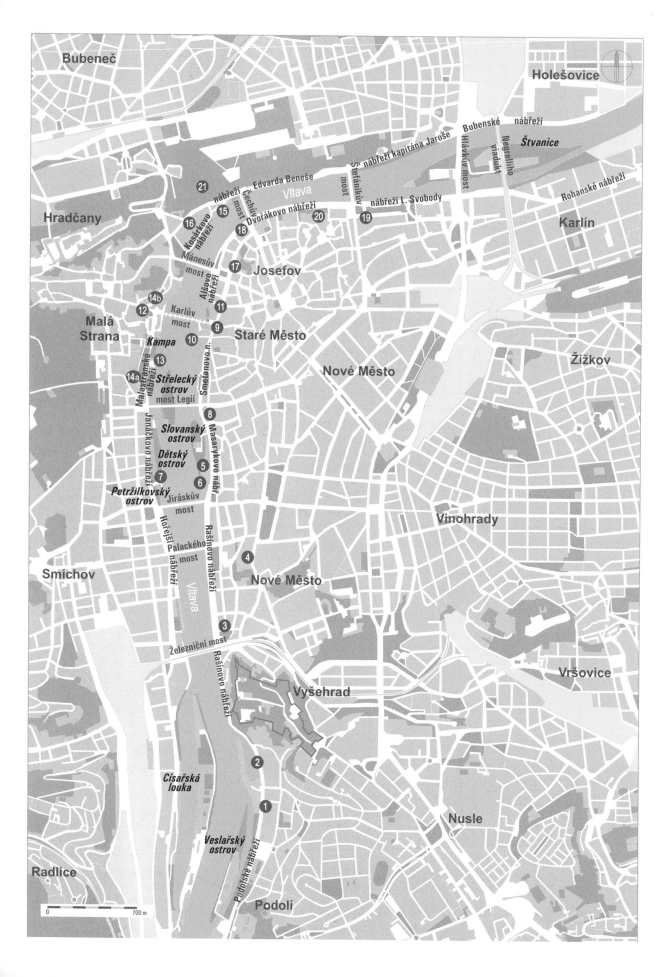

A MAP OF THE PLACES MENTIONED IN THIS BOOK

1. Podolská vodárna (Podolí waterworks)
2. Podolské přístaviště (Podolí port)
3. The customs house at Výtoň (Podskalí)
4. Emauzy (Emmaus Abbey)
5. Mánes Artists Society building
6. Šítkovská vodárenská věž (Šítka Water Tower)
7. Petržílkovská vodárenská věž (Petržílka Water Tower, also known as Lesser Town Water Tower)
8. Národní divadlo (National Theatre)
9. Staroměstská mostecká věž (Bridge Tower on the Old Town side)
10. Staroměstské mlýny a vodárenská věž (Old Town Mills and Old Town Water Tower)
11. Křižovnický klášter (Convent of the Knights of the Cross Convent)
12. Malostranská mostecká věž (Bridge Tower on the Lesser Town side)
13. Sovovy mlýny (Sova Mills)
14a, 14b. Čertovka (Devil's Mill Race)
15. Občanská plovárna (Public Swimming Pool)
16. Strakova akademie (Straka Academy, today the seat of the Czech Government)
17. Rudolfinum (concert halls and art gallery)
18. Právnická fakulta (Law Faculty)
19. Novomlýnská vodárenská věž (New Mills Water Tower)
20. Anežský klášter (Convent of St Agnes)
21. Hanavský pavilon (Hanau Pavilion)

MONARCHS, ARTISTS, ARCHITECTS, BUILDERS, AND POLITICIANS

Agnes of Bohemia (1211–1282), a daughter of King Ottokar I Přemysl; she was the founder of the Order of the Knights of the Cross with the Red Star and also of the Franciscan Convent that today bears her name.

Charles IV (1316–1378), King of Bohemia, Emperor of the Holy Roman Empire, initiator of important Prague building works; during his reign, Prague experienced its greatest efflorescence.

Elizabeth of Bohemia (Eliška Přemyslovna) (1292–1330), the first queen consort of John of Bohemia (of Luxembourg), was a Přemyslid and the mother of the future king and emperor, Charles IV.

Francis I (1768–1835), first Emperor of Austria (and last Emperor of the Holy Roman Empire), King of Hungary and Bohemia, *reg.* 1792–1835.

Francis Joseph I (1830–1916), Emperor of Austria, King of Hungary and Bohemia, *reg.* 1848–1916.

Franz Ferdinand (1863–1914), Archduke of Austria-d'Este, heir to the Austrian throne, assassinated in Sarajevo in 1914.

Joseph II (1741–1790), Emperor of the Holy Roman Empire, King of Bohemia, a proponent of the Enlightenment.

Judith of Thuringia (*c.*1135–1174), Queen of Bohemia, wife of Vladislav II; initiated the building of the first stone bridge over the Vltava.

Libuše, a central figure of Czech mythology; according to legend, together with her husband, Přemysl the Ploughman, was the founder of the Přemyslid dynasty.

Rudolph, crown prince (1858–1889), son of the Emperor Francis Joseph I; heir to the Austrian throne.

Vladislav II (1110–1174), Duke of Bohemia, a Přemyslid, second King of Bohemia (as Vladislav I).

Vratislav II (1033–1092), Duke of Bohemia, a Přemyslid, first King of Bohemia.

Wenceslas (*c.*907–935, previously thought to have died in 929), the major patron saint of the Bohemian Lands, Duke of Bohemia, a Přemyslid.

Wenceslas I (1205–1253), King of Bohemia, son of Ottokar I Přemysl, brother of St Agnes of Bohemia.

Wenceslas II (1271–1305), King of Bohemia, father of Elizabeth of Bohemia.

Wenceslas III (1289–1306), King of Bohemia, last Přemyslid monarch.

Wenceslas IV (1361–1419), King of Bohemia, first-born son of Charles IV.

Aleš, Mikoláš (1852–1913), important Czech painter and illustrator, who in his work sings the praises of the Czech nation.

Alliprandi, Giovanni Battista (*c.*1665–1720), Italian Baroque architect active in Bohemia.

Alt, Rudolf (1812–1905), Austrian painter, maker of topographically accurate cityscapes.

Amena, Tomáš (1867–1937), Czech architect and builder.

Balšánek, Antonín (1865–1921), Czech architect and professor of architecture.

Bělský, Quido (1855–1909), Czech architect, builder, and politician.

Bendl, Johann George (Jan Jiří) (*c*.1610–1680), distinguished Czech sculptor of the Early Baroque period.

Beneš, Edvard (1884–1948), Czechoslovak politician, President of Czechoslovakia from 1935 to 1938 and 1945 to 1948.

Bílek, František (1872–1941), a leading Bohemian sculptor of the Art Nouveau and Symbolist styles.

Braun, Matthias Bernhard (Matyáš Bernard) (1684–1738), Austrian sculptor and woodcarver active in Bohemia; the most important sculptor of the Baroque in Bohemia.

Brokoff, Ferdinand Maximilian (1688–1731), major sculptor and woodcarver of the Baroque in Bohemia.

Brokoff, Johann (1652–1718), sculptor and wood-carver of German origin; father of F. M. Brokoff.

Bruner-Dvořák, Jaroslav (1881–1942), Czech photographer.

Bruner-Dvořák, Rudolf (1864–1921), important Czech photojournalist.

Čapek, Jindřich (1837–1895), Czech sculptor.

Čech, Svatopluk (1846–1908), Czech poet, novelist, and journalist.

Černý, František Maria (1903–1978), Czech architect.

Chochol, Josef (1880–1956), Czech architect, urban planner, and furniture designer, made his name particularly with buildings in the Cubist style.

Cosmas of Prague (*c*.1045–1125), the dean of the Prague Chapter, author of a chronicle of the earliest history and myths of the Bohemian Lands.

Cubr, František (1911–1976), Czech architect and teacher, a founder of the 'Brussels Style' (named after the successful Czechoslovak pavilion at Expo 58).

Dientzenhofer, Kilian Ignaz (1689–1751), architect and builder of German origin; a leading figure of the High Baroque in Bohemia.

Dittrich, František (1801–1875), Podolí raftsman, timber merchant, and Mayor of Prague from 1870 to 1873.

Drahoňovský, Josef (1877–1938), Czech sculptor and gem-cutter.

Dryák, Alois (1872–1932), Czech architect of the Art Nouveau period.

Dufek, Emil (1877–1957), Czech architect.

Dvořák, Antonín (1841–1904), renowned Czech composer.

Dvořák, Karel (1893–1950), Czech sculptor.

Eckert, Jindřich (1833–1905), important Czech photographer.

Engel, Antonín (1879–1958), Czech architect and urban planner.

Fanta, Josef (1856–1954), Czech architect and furniture designer in the Art Nouveau period.

Filsak, Karel (1917–2000), Czech architect.

Fojtík, Josef (1890–1966), Czech sculptor.

Fragner, Jaroslav (1898–1967), Czech modernist architect.

Fridrich, František (1829–1892), the most important Czech photographer of the first period of the medium.

Friedberg (pseud. **Mírohorský**), **Salomon Emanuel** (1821–1908), army officer, painter, and writer.

Gehry Frank Owen (b. 1929), internationally renowned Canadian-born American architect.

Grueber, Bernhard (1807–1882), German architect and art historian, first Professor of Architecture at the Academy of Fine Arts, Prague.

Gutfreund, Otto (1889–1927), Czech sculptor, pioneer of Cubist sculpture.

Hähnel, Ernst Julius (1811–1891), German sculptor and teacher.

Havel, Václav (1936–2011), Czech dramatist, essayist, President of Czechoslovakia (1989–92) and the Czech Republic (1993–2003).

Havel, Vácslav (1861–1921), builder and philanthropist, grandfather of the future president.

Havránek, Bedřich (1821–1899), Czech painter of realistic landscapes.

Hlávka, Josef (1831–1908), Czech architect and builder working throughout Austria-Hungary, was also a major philanthropist.

Hofman, Vlastislav (1884–1964), Czech architect, painter, graphic arts, and set designer.

Hollar, Wenceslaus (1607–1677), Czech engraver and draughtsman active in Germany and England.

Hrubý, Josef (1906–1988), Czech modern architect, co-founder of 'Brussels Style' (named after the successful Czechoslovak pavilion at Expo 58).

Hubička, Stanislav (b. 1930), Czech architect, participated in the design of Prague bridges.

Hübschmann, Bohumil (1878–1961), Czech architect.

Janáček, Leoš (1854–1928), renowned Czech composer.

Janák, Pavel (1882–1956), Czech architect, made his name particularly with buildings in the Cubist style.

Jaroš, Otakar (1912–1943), Czechoslovak Army officer, in the resistance abroad.

Jäckel, Mathias Wenzel (Matěj Václav, in Czech, Maćij Wjacław Jakula, in Sorb) (1655–1738), a sculptor and wood-carver of Sorb origin, active in Bohemia.

Jirásek, Alois (1851–1930), Czech novelist and dramatist.

Kafka, Bohumil (1878–1942), Czech sculptor and teacher at the Academy of Fine Arts.

Klar, Alois (1763–1833), philologist, teacher, founder of the Institute for the Blind in Prague.

Klenka z **Vlastimilu, Richard** (1873–1954), Czech architect.

Klusáček, Karel Ladislav (1865–1929), Czech painter and illustrator.

Kofránek, Ladislav Jan (1880–1954), Czech sculptor in the style of Art Nouveau Symbolism.

Kohl, Ludwig (Ludvík) (1746–1821), Czech painter and draughtsman.

Kosárek, Josef (1830–1859), Czech painter.

Kotěra, Jan (1871–1923), important Czech architect and pioneer of modernist architecture.

Koula, Jan (1855–1919), Czech architect, painter, and designer.

Králíček, Emil (1877–1930), Czech architect working in the Art Nouveau and Cubist styles.

Kramář, Karel (1860–1937), politician, first Premier of the Czechoslovak Republic.

Kranner, Josef (1801–1871), Czech architect working in the Romantic and early Revivalist styles.

Krocín, Václav z Drahobejle (1532–1605), Mayor of the Old Town of Prague.

Kvasnička, Vilém (1885–1969), Czech architect.

Lanna, Vojtěch, Jr (1836–1909), Czech entrepreneur, art collector, philanthropist.

Lanna, Vojtěch, Sr (1805–1866), Czech industrialist, builder, shipbuilder.

Lederer, František Xaver (1758–1811), Prague sculptor in the Empire and Neo-Classical styles.

Lurago, Carlo (1615–1684), Italian Baroque architect working in Bohemia.

Machoň, Ladislav (1888–1973), Czech architect, urban planner, and stage designer.

Machytka, Jan (1844–1887), Czech architect.

Malejovský, Josef (1914–2003), Czech sculptor.

Mánes, Josef (1820–1871), important Czech painter and illustrator, proponent of Czech Romanticism.

Mařatka, Josef (1874–1934), Czech sculptor.

Masaryk, Tomáš Garrigue (1850–1937), philosopher, politician, founder of the modern Czech state; first president of the Czechoslovak Republic (1918–35).

Mathey, Jean-Baptiste (1630–1696), French Baroque architect active in Bohemia.

Matthew of Arras (1290–1352), first master mason of St Vitus' Cathedral.

Mauder, Josef (1854–1920), Czech sculptor and painter.

Max, Emanuel (1810–1901), Bohemian sculptor of German ethnicity.

Max, Josef (1804–1855), Bohemian sculptor of German ethnicity.

Mencl, František (1879–1960), Czech bridge builder and engineer.

Milunić, Vlado (b. 1941), Czech architect of Croat origin.

Mocker, Josef (1835–1899), Czech architect specializing in the restoration of historic buildings.

Morstadt, Vincent (1802–1875), the leading proponent of the Romantic topographically accurate cityscape.

Mosto, Ottavio (1659–1701), Italian Baroque sculptor active also in Bohemia.

Mráček, Konstantín (1859–1931), Czech architect.

Münzberger, Bedřich (1846–1928), Czech architect working in Revival styles.

Myslbek, Josef Václav (1848–1922), important Czech sculptor working in the style of monumental Realism.

Navrátil, Josef (1798–1827), Czech painter, made murals in the Romantic style.

Negrelli, Alois (Luigi) (1799–1858), Austrian transportation engineer specialized in railways; his ideas were influential in the building of the Suez Canal.

Němcová, Božena (1820–1862), Czech writer.

Novák, Józa (1883–1958), Czech sculptor.

Novák, Karel Vratislav (1942–2014), Czech sculptor, particularly kinetic sculpture.

Novotný, Otakar (1880–1959), Czech architect.

Ohmann, Friedrich (1858–1927), Austrian architect active in Bohemia.

Opatrný, Karel (1881–1961), Czech sculptor.

Palach, Jan (1948–1969), a student, set himself on fire on Wenceslas Square to rouse his fellow citizens out of their passivity a year after the Soviet-led military intervention.

Palacký, František (1798–1876), Czech historian and politician.

Parler, Peter (1332–1399), stone mason, sculptor, and most important master mason of St Vitus's Cathedral.

Paukert, Josef (1915–1981), Czech painter and graphic artist.

Pekárek, Josef (1873–1930), Czech sculptor and medallist.

Petrů, Mečislav (1881–1941), Czech architect and head of the building department at City Hall.

Podzemný, Richard (1907–1987), Czech architect and urban-planner, worked in the style of Functionalism.

Pokorný, Karel (1891–1962), Czech sculptor in the Realist style.

Pokorný, Zdeněk (1909–1984), Czech architect and artist.

Popp, Antonín (1850–1915), Czech sculptor and medallist.

Prachner, Václav (1784–1832), Prague sculptor and woodcarver of the Neo-Classical period.

Prager, Karel (1923–2001), Czechoslovak architect and pioneer of modernist architecture in this country.

Rašín, Alois (1867–1923), Czech and Czechoslovak politician, economist, a founding father of Czechoslovakia in 1918.

Rieger, František Ladislav (1818–1903), distinguished Czech politician.

Roith, František (1876–1942), Czech architect.

Roštlapil, Václav (1856–1930), Czech architect working in Revival styles.

Rupp, Wilhelm (1821–1893), German photographer active in Prague in the 1850s and 1860s.

Ruston, Joseph John (1809–1895), British design engineer and shipbuilder, founder of a factory in what is now the Prague district of Karlín.

Sakař, Josef (1856–1936), Czech architect and urban planner.

Sander, František (1871–1932), Czech architect specialized in hydrological engineering.

Schikaneder, Jakub (1855–1924), Czech painter, known particularly for his Prague subject matter.

Schlaffer, František (1855–1924), Czech architect and builder.

Schmoranz, František, Jr (1845–1892), Czech architect and first Director of the Museum of Decorative Arts in Prague.

Schnirch, Bedřich (1791–1868), Czech transportation and design engineer.

Schulz, Josef (1840–1917), Czech architect.

Seifert, Jaroslav (1901–1986), Czech poet and writer, winner of the 1984 Nobel Prize for Literature.

Šimek, Ludvík (1837–1886), Czech sculptor.

Smetana, Bedřich (1824–1884), renowned Czech composer.

Soukup, Jiří (1855–1938), Czech engineer and bridge builder.

Štefánik, Milan Rastislav (1880–1919), Slovak politician.

Štursa, Jan (1880–1925), important Czech sculptor in the style of Art Nouveau Symbolism.

Štursa, Jiří (1910–1995), Czech architect and urban planner.

Sudek, Josef (1896–1976), one of the most famous Czech photographers.

Sucharda, Stanislav (1866–1916), Czech sculptor and medallist.

Švec, Otakar (1892–1955), Czech sculptor.

Šverma, Jan (1901–1944), Czech Communist journalist and politician.

Svoboda, Ludvík (1895–1979), Czechoslovak general and politician, President of Czechoslovakia from 1968 to 1975.

Thomayer, František Josef (1856–1938), important Czech landscape architect.

Ullmann, Vojtěch Ignác (1822–1897), Czech architect.

Velich, František (1866–1923), Czech architect.

Vosmík, Čeněk (1860–1944), Czech sculptor and restorer of historic works of sculpture.

Wagner, Antonín Pavel (1934–1895), Czech sculptor, worked mostly in Vienna.

Wagner, Jan (1941–2005), Czech sculptor, son of Josef Wagner.

Wagner, Josef (1901–1957), Czech sculptor.

Wiehl, Antonín (1846–1910), Czech architect working only in Revivalist styles.

Wimmer, Jakub (1754–1822), Prague businessman and philanthropist.

Wurzel, Ludvík (1865–1913), Czech sculptor.

Zasche, Josef (1871–1957), Bohemian-born architect.

Ženíšek, František (1849–1916), Czech Realist painter.

Zeyer, Jan (1847–1903), Czech architect.

Zítek, Josef (1832–1909), the most important Czech architect of the Neo-Renaissance style.

Zobel, Josef Klement (1746–1814), Czech architect and builder.

LIST OF ILLUSTRATIONS

Dust jacket:
Prague – bridges over the Vltava (front); an arch of Charles Bridge (back)
Dust-jacket flap:
The Tower on the Old Town end of Charles Bridge
Pages 2-12:
Charles Bridge (double-page spread)
Prague panorama
The National Theatre
Allegory of the Vltava, Dětský ostrov (Children's Island)
Bruncvík/Roland statue on Charles Bridge

I. Documentary photographs
(The photos on pp. 14–41 and 44 come from the collections of the City of Prague Museum)

Joris Hoefnagel and Abraham Hogenberg, *View of Prague from 1572*, hand-coloured copper engraving, from *Civitates orbis terrarum* (1598), p. 14.
Rudolf Alt and F. X. Sandmann, *At the Old Town Mills*, hand-coloured lithograph, *c.*1840, p. 15.
Bedřich Havránek, *Between the New Mills and the Helm Mills*, watercolour, *c.*1850, p. 15.
Václav Kroupa, *Sand Miners Upstream from* Šítka *Weir, oil on canvas, 1884*, p. 16.
Salomon Emanuel Friedberg-Mírohorský, *The Riverbank at Smíchov upstream from the Lesser Town Waterworks*, oil on canvas, 1886, p. 17.
Vincenc Morstadt and Václav Merklas, *The Krocín Fountain*, steel engraving, 1847, p. 18.
Wilhelm Rupp, *Podskalí from the North,* photograph, *c.*1865, p. 20.
Podskalí from the South, photograph, unknown photographer, *c.*1900, p. 21.
Jindřich Eckert, *Ice Harvesting*, photograph, *c.*1895, p. 22.
Ludvík Kohl and Josef Gregory, *The Old Town Weir*, hand-coloured copper engraving, 1793, p. 23.
Karlín Port, oil on canvas, unknown artist, *c.*1850, p. 24.
The Na Františku Wharves, photograph, unknown photographer, *c.*1865, p. 25.
Jindřich Eckert, *The Francis I Bridge*, photograph, before 1898, p. 26.
František Fridrich, *The Francis Joseph I Bridge,* photograph, *c.*1870, p. 26.
František Fridrich, *The Iron Footbridge*, photograph, *c.*1870, p. 27.
First Steamboat on the Vltava, lithograph, unknown artist, 1841, p. 29.
Jindřich Eckert, *The Steamboat* Praha/Prag, photograph, 1865, p. 30.
F. J. Trojan, *The Steamboat* Primátor Dittrich, photograph, *c.*1908, p. 30.
Jaroslav Bruner-Dvořák, *At the Smíchov Lock*, photograph, 1931, p. 31.
Jan Novotný, *Sand Barges*, photograph, *c.*1955, p. 32.

II. Exteriors

15 A, B/ Slav Island (Slovanský ostrov); Monument to Božena Němcová

16 A, B/ Petržilka Water Tower and Weir

17A–G/ Janáček Embankment (Janáčkovo nábřeží); Smíchov Lock

18/ Children's Island (Dětský ostrov)

19/ Lesser Town Embankment (Malostranské nábřeží)

20 A, B/ Sharpshooter Island (Střelecký ostrov)

21 A, B/ Bridge of the Legions (Most Legií)

22 A, B/ National Theatre (Národní divadlo)

23 A, B/ Smetana Embankment (Smetanovo nábřeží)

24/ Old Town Mills and Water Tower (Staroměstské mlýny and Staroměstská věž)

25 A, B/ Knights of the Cross Square (Křižovnické náměstí); Church of St Saviour (Kostel Nejsvětějšího Salvátora); Church of St Francis of Assisi (Kostel sv. Františka Serafínského); Old Town Bridge Tower (Staroměstská mostecká věž)

26 A–F/ Charles Bridge (Karlův most); St John Nepomucene; St Ludmila; Bruncvík/ Roland

27/ Lesser Town end of Charles Bridge

28 A–E/ Kampa Island; Lichtenstein House (Lichtenštejnský palác); On Kampa; Sova Mills (Sovovy mlýny)

29 A–D/ Prague Venice (Pražské Benátky); Herget Brickyard (Hergetova cihelna)

30/ Aleš Embankment (Alšovo nábřeží)

31A–D/ Mánes Bridge (Mánesův most); Mánes statue in park at Old Town end; Klárov

32 A, B/ Straka Academy (Strakova akademie) – Office of the Government; Public Swimming Pool (Občanská plovárna)

33 A–C/ Jan Palach Square (Náměstí Jana Palacha); Faculty of Arts, Charles University; Rudolfinum; panorama of Prague Castle

34 A–C/ Dvořák Embankment (Dvořákovo nábřeží); Faculty of Law, Charles University

35 A–C/ Čech Bridge (Čechův most); Chapel of St Mary Magdalene (Kaple sv. Máří Magdaleny)

36/ Na Františku; Agnes Convent (Anežský klášter)

37 A–B/ Štefánik Bridge (Štefánikův most)

38/ New Mills Water Tower (Novomlýnská vodárenská věž)

39 A, B/ St Peter Embankment (Petrské nábřeží); power station on Štvanice Island

40 A–D/ Hlávka Bridge (Hlávkův most)

41 A–D/ Letná Park (Letenské sady); Hanau Pavilion (Hanavský pavilon); Prague Metronome

42/ Prague bridges from Letná Park

KATEŘINA BEČKOVÁ

From an early age, Kateřina Bečková has had an intense interest in old Prague and the literature about it, particularly the five-volume series *Zmizelá Praha* (Lost Prague), published by Václav Poláček from 1946 to 1948. After graduating from secondary school, in 1977, she quite naturally headed for the City of Prague Museum, where she worked part-time while studying Cultural Studies at Charles University. After graduating, in 1982, she was made the curator of the Museum's Collection of Historical Photographs and the Langweil Model of Prague, and has remained at the job to this day. She has published mostly on architectural and urban change in nineteenth and twentieth-century Prague. Since 2000, she has been the Chairman of the Society for the Preservation of Old Prague (Klub Za starou Prahu).

At the City of Prague Museum, she organized an exhibition of the Langweil model of Prague (1982–83), an exhibition to mark the 200th anniversary of Antonín Langweil, who made the model (1991–92), an exhibition to mark the 100th anniversary of the laws for the clearance and renewal of the Jewish quarter (1993–94), an exhibition to mark the 650th anniversary of the founding of the New Town of Prague (1998), and an exhibition to mark the 200th anniversary of the birth of the artist Vincenc Morstadt (2002). At the Waldstein Riding School, she organized an exhibition about Prague architecture that has been demolished (2000–01).

Apart from her first book in English, *Lost Prague: The City's Historic Centre*, trans. Gita Zbavitelová (Litomyšl and Prague: Paseka and Schola ludus–Pragensia, 2007), and the current book, her publications include the following:

'Asanace – zatracovaný i obdivovaný projekt obce Pražské', in *Pražská asanace: K 100. výročí vydání asanačního zákona pro Prahu*, Prague: Acta musei pragensis, 1993.
Svědectví Langweilova modelu Prahy, Prague: Muzeum hlavního města Prahy and Schola ludus–Pragensia, 1996.
Zmizelá Praha: Nové Město, Prague: Schola ludus–Pragensia, 1998.
'Sto let Klubu Za starou Prahu v sedmi kapitolách', in *Sto let Klubu Za starou Prahu 1900–2000*, Prague: Klub Za starou Prahu, 2000.
Zmizelá Praha: Hradčany a Malá Strana, Prague: Schola ludus–Pragensia, 2000.
Zmizelá Praha: Dodatky I. Historický střed města, Prague and Litomyšl: Paseka, 2003.
Zmizelá Praha: Dodatky II. Historická předměstí a okraje města – pravý břeh Vltavy, Prague and Litomyšl: Paseka, 2003.
Zmizelá Praha: Dodatky III. Historická předměstí a okraje města – levý břeh Vltavy, Prague and Litomyšl: Paseka, 2004.
Zmizelá Praha: Staré Město, Prague: Paseka and Schola ludus–Pragensia, 2005.

'Malá Strana a její radnice', in *Malostranská beseda a její znovuzrození*, Prague: Práh, 2009.

Zmizelá Praha: Nádraží a železniční tratě. Zaniklé proměněné a ohrožené stavby, Prague: Paseka and Schola ludus–Pragensia, 2009.

Zmizelá Praha: Továrny a tovární haly. Pt 1: *Vysočany, Libeň, Karlín*. Prague: Paseka and Schola ludus–Pragensia, 2011.

Zmizelá Praha: Továrny a tovární haly. Pt 2: *Smíchov, Jinonice, Holešovice a další čtvrti na levém břehu Vltavy*, Prague: Paseka, Schola ludus–Pragensia, 2012.

'"Ztracený ráj" na Langweilově modelu Prahy: Malované prospekty měšťanských zahrad', *Historica Pragensia* 5, Prague: Muzeum hlavního města Prahy, 2013.

Zmizelá Praha: Továrny a tovární haly. Pt 3: *Žižkov, Vinohrady, Nusle, Modřany a další čtvrti na levém břehu Vltavy*, Prague: Paseka and Schola ludus–Pragensia, 2014.

This series is devoted to the history of Prague, with a focus on the arts and intellectual life of the city. In a factual yet lively way it seeks to give an informed account of the thousand-year development of the city with its changes, both intellectual and material, and its legendary *genius loci*, thus contributing to general knowledge about Czech culture.

A typical volume in the series comprises a comprehensive account of the topic, accompanied by illustrations and 'walks through Prague', by means of photographs of the preserved historic architecture and other works of art together with commentary. The publication includes a list of important historical figures, an index with corresponding maps of the location of the art and architecture, and a bibliography.

The contributors to this series are respected Prague art historians, photographers, and translators.